Journey
FOR CHILDKEN

Leader's
Guide

Author:
Francine M. O'Connor

Art and design:
Wendy Barnes

ISBN 0-7648-0160-0
Library of Congress Catalog Card Number: 98-067153
03 04 05 06 07   7 6 5 4 3

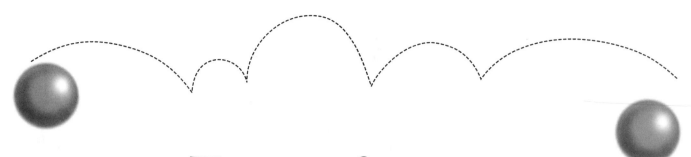

Table of Contents

(For a detailed history of the catechumenate process, see *Journey of Faith* Leader's Book)

 The Process

The catechumenate is rightly called a *process*, rather than a program. Catechists and sponsors guide the spiritual journey of adults and children. It varies according to time, place, and needs of the catechumens. The process is one of faith development. Catechumens grow in their relationship with God, as expressed through Roman Catholic beliefs. The process nourishes relationships between catechumens, catechists, and the parish community.

Inquiry

The first stage of the faith journey is called the *inquiry*. Sessions are informal and center on the life stories that brought each member to this time and place. Questions about faith, God, and God's love are considered. There is ample opportunity to ask questions related to *things Catholic*.

The set of twelve *Journey of Faith for Children* Inquiry handouts assist the children through this period. They cover basic questions in the areas of Catholic belief, Mass, the Bible, saints, prayer, and practices.

This is a time for inquirers to learn the ways Catholics worship together and how they bring their Christian faith to life. First impressions of the parish community and those involved with the catechumenate process are important. This stage culminates with the commitment to enter the catechumenate, to prepare for entrance into full membership with the Catholic Church.

Catechumenate

To mark the beginning of the catechumenate is the *Rite of Becoming a Catechumen*. At this point, *inquirers* become *catechumens* (preparing for baptism) or *candidates* (already baptized but preparing for membership in the Church). They publicly state their wish to continue the process of formation, and the community commits their prayerful support. Selected members of the parish community join the process as sponsors and lend their support to the catechumens and candidates.

During this phase, catechesis may take place during the Sunday liturgy. If it does, the catechumens and candidates are dismissed after the *Prayers of the Faithful*. Catechists and sponsors, join them in reflecting on the readings for the day and connecting the Scripture to the faith life of the Church. *Journey of Faith* Leader's and Participant's books will be invaluable aids in this process. The 16 Catechumenate handouts aid in the learning process, addressing the specifics of our faith: Church, sacraments, moral life, etc.

The length of this stage is determined by the needs of the catechumen/candidate and the community. It can last anywhere from several months to three years. During this time, catechumens and candidates are exposed to various forms of prayer; they worship with the community, participate in the apostolic life of the Church, and join in community actions.

When they are ready to make a formal request for the sacraments of initiation, and when the catechists and sponsors are ready to recommend them to the bishop and the parish for full membership, the *Rite of Election* is celebrated. This rite is held at the cathedral on the first Sunday of Lent and marks the closure of the catechumenate and the beginning of the *Period of Enlightenment*, the time to prepare for the sacraments of initiation at the Easter Vigil on Holy Saturday.

Lent

The beginning of Lent signals a 40-day retreat in which the parish community joins those who have been *elected* for full membership *(the elect)* in preparation for the Easter Vigil. On the third, fourth, and fifth Sundays, the *Rites of the Scrutinies* are celebrated during the liturgy. In these prayers, the elect and the faithful are reminded of the need of continued healing, conversion, and reconciliation. Sessions are marked by increased emphasis on prayer rather than on accumulation of knowledge. Aiding the catechists in this process is a series of eight Lent handouts, which focus on the Easter Vigil and preparation for reception of the sacraments of initiation. Many parishes allow time during Lent for a day of prayer designed for the elect and their sponsors.

Mystagogy

The Easter Vigil marks the beginning of a commitment to a lifelong discovery of the Christian message. The 50 days from Easter to Pentecost are called the period of *mystagogy*, a Greek word meaning mystery. The post-Easter period serves as a time for the neophytes, or beginners, to form a closer relationship with one another and come to a deeper understanding of God's Word and the sacraments. They continue to gather, but the sessions now center the apostolic or social justice aspects of Catholic Christianity. Eight Mystagogy handouts help redirect the focus of new Catholics from learning to living. Neophytes are invited to participate in parish life so their faith may continue to be nourished.

The Catechumenate and the Community

The catechumenate process provides a means of renewal for the entire parish community. It is a constant reminder of our roots, heritage, and traditions. Each beginning offers an opportunity for all to re-enter the path of faith, share the life story of God-with-us, and grow into a mature relationship with God and one another.

 The Methods

Suggestions for Developing a Catechumenate Process

Catechists are encouraged to use their judgment in developing a process of faith formation suited to the needs of catechumens and candidates. (The materials presented here acts as guides and aids to that end.) Pay special attention to the section entitled *Leader Meditation.* This is a chance for you to focus on your own spirituality. Sometimes, specific readings have been designated for your preparation.

Though one doesn't have to be a theology professor or an experienced teacher to be a successful catechist, there are techniques and practical suggestions that can make the experience easier and more enjoyable. While a faith-filled experience is the work of God, it takes planning on the part of the catechumenate team to ensure that the process goes smoothly. It's helpful for all to review the materials prior to the first session.

The team should meet monthly throughout the process. It is helpful if each catechist is aware of topics discussed, materials covered, and questions raised in each session to assure continuity between sessions and among presenters. It is also advisable that catechists contact the following week's presenters to brief them on issues that may need to be addressed.

No one can predict the makeup of any particular group. You may have some children who have had no contact with institutionalized religion, some who were baptized and active in another Christian denomination, and still others who were baptized Catholic but not raised in the Church. Generally all of the students can participate in the same sessions; the major difference will come in the celebration of the rites (see the *Rites* for specific instructions in this regard).

Communication and active listening are the catechist's greatest tool in establishing a sense of trust among participants. Active listening requires *empathy and sensitivity* — an acceptance of the uniqueness of each individual, an understanding of other's feelings, and a willingness to control one's own prejudice and emotions. It requires *attentiveness* — the ability to look at the person and give undivided attention and *receptiveness* — the genuine desire to hear and be open to what is said.

> Note to Leaders: Each of the student handouts includes two blank pages entitled My Space. This space was designated for notetaking or whatever the child chooses. If needed, you can use the space for the group activities.

 The Rites

Rite of Acceptance Into the Order of Catechumens

This rite marks the first important transition in one's journey of faith — the move from being an interested inquirer to becoming a catechumen. The importance of this step in one's life is rightly recognized by the Church. Sponsors should have been chosen prior to this rite. If the catechumen doesn't have a sponsor in mind, an appropriate person can be selected from a pool of parish volunteers.

Symbolizing movement into the community, those asking to be received as catechumens, along with their sponsors, usually begin the journey at the doors of the Church (Rite 48). The celebrant introduces them to the worshiping community, asking, "What do you ask of the Church?" They state their desire for initiation, implying their intent to live, learn, and love with the community. The Sign of the Cross is marked on each forehead, symbolizing the love and strength of Christ that accompanies each person (Rite 54-55).

This Sign may also be marked on their ears, that they may hear the voice of the Lord; on their eyes, that they may see God's glory; on their lips, that they may bear the gentle yoke of Christ; on their hands, that their work may witness Christ; and on their feet, that they may walk in Christ's way (see Rite 56). At the conclusion of the Signing, catechumens and sponsors are formally invited to enter the Church and to join in the celebration of the Liturgy of the Word (Rite 60).

Following the readings and homily, it is recommended that the catechumens be called forward and presented with a book of the gospels or a cross (Rite 64). They are included in the community's intercessory prayers before being formally dismissed from the assembly to pray and reflect on the Scriptures (see Rite 65-67).

For those seeking full communion in the Church who are already baptized (candidates), the Rite of Welcoming Baptized but Previously Uncatechized Adults Who Are Preparing for Confirmation and/or Eucharist or Reception into the Full Communion of the Catholic Church is to be used. (See Rite 507 and following, Appendix 1, for integrating both candidates and catechumens into the introductory celebration rite.)

Rites of the Catechumenate

Other liturgical rites may take place during the catechumenate: celebrations of the Word of God (Rite 81-89); minor exorcisms (Rite 90-93); blessings (Rite 95-96); anointing (Rite 98-101); sending (Rite 106-117). These rites, although optional, are important for the continuing faith development of the catechumens/candidates and the parish community.

Rite of Election

The importance of this rite is accented by the fact that it's celebrated by the bishop (or bishop's representative), generally on the first Sunday of Lent. The rite marks another transition — one duly noted by a change of title from catechumen to elect. Godparents and/or sponsors have been chosen and approved.

After those requesting election have been presented to the bishop (Rite 130) and approved by the entire people of God there present (Rite 131), their names are inscribed in the Book of Enrollment (Rite 132). Intercessory prayers and a special blessing for all the elect follow this sacred moment.

Rites of the Scrutinies

The First Scrutiny takes place on the Third Sunday of Lent. Its focus is the gospel of the woman at the well. After special intercessory prayers, the celebrant prays that the elect may be exorcized from the power of sin (Rite 150-156). During the week that follows, the Presentation of the Creed should be formally made to the elect, preferably after the homily within Mass (Rite 157-163).

The Second Scrutiny takes place on the Fourth Sunday of Lent. Its focus is the gospel of the man born blind. Again, after intercessory prayers, the celebrant prays that the elect may be exorcized from the powers of sin (Rite 164-170).

The Fifth Sunday of Lent brings the Third Scrutiny. This Sunday focuses on the raising of Lazarus. Intercessory prayers from all the community and prayers of exorcism from the celebrant again follow (Rite 171-177). During the week after this rite, the Presentation of the Lord's Prayer should be formally made to the elect, preferably after the reading of the Gospel of the Lord's Prayer according to Matthew. Following the homily, which centers on the meaning and importance of the Lord's Prayer, the celebrant calls on the worshiping community to silently pray for all the elect. Before their dismissal, the celebrant bestows a special blessing upon the elect (Rite 178-184).

Rites of Preparation

When it's possible to bring the elect together on Holy Saturday for reflection and prayer, these rites may be considered for use in immediate preparation for the reception of the sacraments (Rite 185 and following). If either the Presentation of the Creed or the

Presentation of the Lord's Prayer has not been celebrated already, they could be included now. An *Ephphetha Rite* (opening ears and mouth to symbolize the hearing and proclaiming of the Word) is a fitting preparation rite, as is the rite of *Choosing a Baptismal Name.* Any or all of these rites set the stage for the highlight of the catechumenate experience — the reception of the sacraments of initiation.

Rites of Initiation

Months of sharing the journeys of faith of the elect, the sponsors, and their catechists culminate in this very special parish celebration. Holy Saturday is the night to celebrate, and the Church celebrates in style. In the early Church the Easter Vigil lasted until dawn; today's Vigil lasts but a few hours (between two and four). It is the most glorious celebration of the entire liturgical year.

This night begins in total darkness. The parish community may assemble outside for the blessing of the fire. As the celebrant processes into the church, proclaiming the *Light of Christ,* each person lights a taper from the new Easter candle that has been ignited with the new fire. Soon the Church is aglow with tongues of new fire. The Liturgy of the Word begins with only the light of the candles. There are seven readings from the Hebrew Scriptures provided for the occasion, although it is not necessary to proclaim all seven. Psalms are interspersed between each reading.

With the singing of the *Gloria,* the altar candles and electric lights are lit and the Church bells are joyously rung. Then comes the New Testament epistle, the glorious *Alleluia,* the gospel, and the homily. The stage is set for the rites of initiation!

The liturgy of baptism begins with the calling forth of those to be baptized. A litany of the saints follows, and then the celebrant blesses the baptismal water by plunging the Easter candle into the pool. Baptism follows, and each of the newly baptized is clothed with a white garment. Then the whole assembly renews their baptismal vows, and the celebrant ritually sprinkles all with the newly blessed waters of baptism.

Once the baptismal rite is concluded, candidates for reception are called forward to profess their belief in the holy Catholic Church. They are joined by the newly baptized, and the rite of confirmation is celebrated with laying on of hands and anointing with chrism.

As the initiation rites conclude and the eucharistic prayer for Holy Saturday begins, new Catholics take the place of the catechumens and candidates who worked and prayed so hard in preparation for this night. They, their sponsors, godparents, and family members lead the Church to the festive eucharistic banquet. The goal of initiation is this Eucharist — sharing at the table and being sent forth.

Alleluia! Amen

 Materials

You will need many materials to make the journey complete. Most of the items can be found in and around the household. These items can be modified according to the age of your group. Here is a list of the supplies you will need:

Rocks, small to medium size
Photos of kids
Instant camera
Old holiday cards
String/yarn
Cardboard (brown and white)
Construction paper
Index cards
Paper (8 ¹/₂" x 11")
Posterboards
Scissors
Crayons, permanent markers
Watercolors
Paper punch
Baby doll and dress
Bowl
Oil
Foam wreaths
Easter supplies — grass, eggs, chicks, bunnies
Florist wire
Tacky glue
Safety pins
Bandages
Hangers
Craft sticks
Wooden and gold crosses
Loaf of bread
Bottle of grape juice
Children's Bible
Candles
Tape — transparent and masking

• Lesson One •
Journey of Faith

"Faith is a gift of God, a supernatural virtue infused by [God]" (*Catechism of the Catholic Church*, #153).

Leader Meditation

A reading from John 14:1.

After meditating on this Scripture passage, try a personal *Faith Check*. When you pray, do you truly believe your prayers are being heard? Do you trust they will be answered? The better you understand your own faith, the easier it will be to transfer this
to the children.

Preparation

Even Jesus understood that we sometimes have doubts, which can help, in an odd way, the growth of our faith. Faith grows just as minds and bodies grow — a little at a time.

Prepare your *Faith Journey Map*. Tape four poster boards together lengthwise. Use this map in your activity section throughout the Inquiry sessions. Scatter the following words on the map, leaving room for the children to add their own creative work under each heading: Faith; We Believe; At Mass; God's Memory Book; Understanding God's Word; The Saints; Mary; Our Church; Church People; Prayer; Tradition; We are the Church.

Scripture Sharing

Select a special area of the room as a Scripture Sharing area. If possible, set up the area away from activity centers. There will be fewer distractions this way. Place chairs in a circle or have a carpeted area where the children can sit in a circle on the floor.

Choose one of the Scripture passages from page two of the handout or read Genesis 22:1-16. If the children are very young, tell the story in your own words. Older children can be selected to do part or all of the reading. Encourage the children to share their feelings about the passage.

Discussion

• Using the questions on page one of the leaflet, discuss people we trust in our everyday life. Why do we trust these particular people? How do we know we can trust them? What happens when someone we trust lets us down?

• We can be sure that God will never disappoint us. This is a promise Jesus made to us in the Bible. Ask the children to share stories of times they prayed for something. Were their prayers answered? If they don't think so, see if you can help them sort out why they feel that God didn't give them an answer.

• Discuss the four ways to help your faith grow stronger. How does reading about God help your faith grow? What about praying or doing good works? Loving others?

Faith Journey Activity

Have the children illustrate a Scripture story that reminds them of faith. They can use the story you read in your Scripture Sharing or one they remember themselves. Tape their drawings in the space near the word *Faith* on the *Faith Journey Map*. Since you will be removing their work at a later time, be sure to use a minimum of tape. (Masking tape is easier to remove.)

> ### *Answer to Rebus is FAITH.*

• Lesson Two •
What Do Catholics Believe?

"*The Apostles' Creed* is so called because it is rightly considered to be a faithful summary of the apostles' faith. It is the ancient baptismal symbol of the Church of Rome. Its great authority arises from this fact: it is 'the Creed of the Roman Church, the See of Peter, the first of the apostles, to which he brought the common faith'" (*Catechism of the Catholic Church,* #194).

Leader Meditation

The Apostles' Creed

I believe in God, the Father almighty, creator of heaven and earth.

I believe in Jesus Christ, God's only Son, our Lord.

He was conceived by the power of the Holy Spirit and born of the Virgin Mary.

He suffered under Pontius Pilate, was crucified, died, and was buried.

He descended to the dead.

On the third day he rose again.

He ascended into heaven, and is seated at the right hand of the Father.

He will come again to judge the living and the dead.

I believe in the Holy Spirit, the holy catholic Church, the communion of saints, the forgiveness of sins, the resurrection of the body, and life everlasting. Amen

 ## Preparation

Read the Apostles' Creed slowly, one line at a time. Picture each faith belief in your mind. Imagine God creating the world for you; Jesus' birth, suffering, death, and Resurrection. Consider the love promise contained within the prayer of our faith. After reading each line, repeat the prayer, "Jesus, I believe. Help my unbelief." One by one, renew your own faith in each truth.

Bring in pictures depicting the different truths in the Creed: the world, Jesus, Mary, saints, crosses, heaven, Holy Spirit. Some good sources include: greeting cards from Easter and Christmas, a children's book of Bible stories, or small holy cards.

 ## Scripture Sharing

Our Creed comes to us directly from the apostles. As background, read or tell of the commissioning of the apostles: Matthew 10:2-31. As you read, have the children imagine they are one of the apostles, listening to Jesus telling them the things that are to come. After the story, let them discuss how they felt about the tasks ahead.

 ## Discussion

• After the children list things they already believe about God, encourage them to talk about why they believe these particular truths.

• Go over the words of the Creed line by line, as is done in the leaflet. Encourage discussion of each line, using ideas that the children can identify with.

• Ask the children if they can name some of the holy days that remind us of our beliefs in the Creed. (Lent, Easter, Christmas, etc.) Can they think of a story from the Bible that tells about one or more of the truths? (Creation, the Annunciation, etc.)

• How does saying the Creed help us to keep God's love in our hearts?

 ## Faith Journey Activity

Using the pictures you brought in, have the children tape a picture for each of the truths found in the creed near the words *We Believe.*

· Lesson Three ·
What Is the Meaning of the Mass?

"It was above all on 'the first day of the week,' Sunday, the day of Jesus' resurrection, that the Christians met 'to break bread.' From that time on down to our own day the celebration of the Eucharist has been continued so that today we encounter it everywhere in the Church with the same fundamental structure. It remains the center of the Church's life" (*Catechism of the Catholic Church*, #1343).

Leader Meditation
A reading from Luke 22:14-20.

 Preparation

We hear the words of today's Scripture every time we go to Mass. Read them now as if you're actually hearing them from Jesus. Picture him sharing the bread and the wine with you personally. Knowing the suffering that's to come, what are your feelings? Since the Eucharist is central to the Mass and to our faith, it would be a good idea to attend Mass shortly before beginning this lesson.

• Prepare a play based on Luke 22:14-28. Make a copy for each child. Highlight quotes from Jesus in different colors to ensure that each child has a chance to "be Jesus."

• Draw or cut out pictures of the Mass for the children to add to their Journey Map.

 Scripture Sharing

For your Scripture Sharing this week, choose the gospel story from next week's Mass. Read from the Bible or an age-appropriate translation. Tell them that this story will be read next week at Mass. Encourage them to listen for it and try to remember when they heard it. Who told the story? What did they learn from the homily following the gospel?

This is an assignment for them to prepare for next week's class.

 Discussion

• Ask the children to take a few minutes to think about the last time they were at Mass. Then give each child a sheet of paper to write down three things they remember from Mass.

• Go over each section of the Mass as outlined in the leaflet. Discuss the answers they wrote for the questions.

• Since, as Inquirers, they will probably not be in attendance for the Eucharist, spend extra time discussing the importance of the Mass.

• Go to your Scripture Sharing area and relive the institution of the Lord's Supper using your play sheets. Tell them that they will take turns being Jesus speaking to the apostles.

 Faith Journey Activity

Tape Mass pictures under the heading *At Mass*. Ask the children if they know what is happening in each picture. Write their descriptions of Mass below each picture.

· Lesson Four ·
The Bible

"*Sacred Scripture* is the speech of God as it is put down in writing under the breath of the Holy Spirit" (*Catechism of the Catholic Church*, #81).

Leader Meditation
Prayer Before Reading the Bible

O God, may your words remain with me,
in my mind, on my lips, and in my heart.
Dancing before my sorrow or joy,
may their message of love not depart.

For every joy has been written,
and every sorrow has been consoled
by your holy Word, forever preserved,
as each chapter and verse unfold.

Preparation

Sit in a comfortable chair and rest your hands in your lap. Choose your favorite Scripture passage. After praying for inspiration, read it slowly. Now, close your eyes and imagine yourself in the passage you just read. Let the images sink into your heart. Remain with them as long as you are comfortable with the silence. Then slowly return to your Scripture passage and read it once again, followed by a prayer.

 Scripture Sharing

Ask the children to take turns telling you a story choosing any passage from Scripture. They can tell it in their own words or, with your help, find and read it in the Bible. After each story, ask the storyteller why that particular passage was chosen.

 Discussion

• Encourage a discussion about family photograph albums. Ask the children what other things the family saves and where these items are kept. Don't rush this discussion. The children need to fully grasp the importance of handing down memories of significant events.

• On the board, outline several important God "memories" from the Bible — Creation, Noah and the flood, Abraham and Sarah, Jacob and the twelve tribes of Israel, David, the birth of Jesus, the miracles, the crucifixion, the Resurrection.

• Discuss the difference between the Old and New Testament. What important event separates the two?

• Give the children a short quiet time to read one of the suggested passages, or select one yourself to tell them.

 Faith Journey Activity

Have the children illustrate their favorite Bible story. Tape their work under the heading *God's Memory Book.*

• Lesson Five •
How Do Catholics Interpret the Bible?

"Sacred Scripture must be read and interpreted in the light of the same Spirit by whom it was written" (*Catechism of the Catholic Church*, #111 — see also #112–114).

 Preparation

For today's lesson, cut out a string of hearts connected together, accordion style. You will need four large hearts or eight smaller ones on your heart-chain. Add the following words to the hearts — a group of two small or one large heart per phrase (God's Word — brings us closer — to one another — and to God), or the children can print the words onto the hearts themselves during class activity time.

 Scripture Sharing

Do the *Pray, Listen, Hear* exercise from the front page of the children's leaflet. Read, or have the children read, the story of Jairus' daughter (Luke 8:40-56) from the Bible. Do not tell it in your own words. It will be important to the exercise that they hear the passage as it is written.

Discussion

• Go over the points from the exercise one at a time. Give the children plenty of time to think about and discuss their ideas. Remember, there are no right or wrong answers for these ideas. This is just an exercise that will teach them to think about what they hear.

• Read and discuss the paragraphs on page two of the leaflet. Ask the children to discuss their favorite Bible stories. Ask, "What is God saying to you in this story?" or "How does this story relate to you?"

• During group time, allow the children to ask about any Bible passages that trouble them. If the passage is one that you don't understand yourself, don't pretend to know. Tell the children that you will bring that passage to someone who does understand and you'll explain it at the next session. It's good for the children to know that even adults don't always understand.

 Faith Journey Activity

Spread out the heart-links so the children can work on them together. Let some of the older children glue or paste the letters across the top of the hearts. Have the other children illustrate the heart below each group of words. Tape the heart-links under the headline *Understanding God's Word.*

• Lesson Six • The Saints

"In prayer, the pilgrim Church is associated with that of the saints, whose intercession she asks" (*Catechism of the Catholic Church,* #2692 — see also #2683, #2684).

Leader Meditation

Lord Jesus, I remember your promise, "I will not leave you orphans." You have sent your Holy Spirit to be with us, to guide us, to lead us to heaven. All who are filled with your Spirit are with us in the communion of saints. Grant that I may always recognize their presence among us and be guided toward holiness and sanctity by their stories and their example. Help me to encourage the children in my care to seek out and follow the examples of those whom you have sent to teach us and to lead us. Amen

 Preparation

Today you will need a half sheet of white construction paper for each child. You will also need a book on the lives of the saints for your *Scripture Sharing* time, preferably one that is age-appropriate. If you don't own an instant camera, ask the child to bring photographs of themselves for the next lesson.

 Scripture Sharing

From your book of saints, choose one the children can follow. The three saints mentioned in the leaflet would be ideal choices. Other choices might be the children of Fatima or Bernadette of Lourdes.

 Discussion

• Ask each child to share who their favorite hero is. Why is this person a hero?

• Read and discuss the saint stories on page two of the leaflet, if they differ from your passages. Mention people you see every day who are saints. Encourage the children to name people they know who also follow God's word faithfully.

• Ask the children to name two or three things they can do in their family life, in the classroom, or with their friends to emulate the saints. Note these things for use during your activity time.

Faith Journey Activity

Give each child a half sheet of white construction paper. Have them draw self portraits following an example of one of the saints they heard about today, leaving some room at the top of the paper. When the drawings are done, ask each child what he or she is doing in the picture. Have them print "Saint (child's name) follows the saints by (washing dishes, playing fair, etc.)" at the top of their self portraits. Tape the pictures on your *Faith Journey Map* under *The Saints*.

• Lesson Seven •
Mary

"Mary's role in the Church is inseparable from her union with Christ and flows directly from it. 'This union of the mother with the Son in the work of salvation is made manifest from the time of Christ's virginal conception up to his death'" (*Catechism of the Catholic Church*, #964 — see #963–975).

Leader Meditation
A reading from Luke 1:46-50.

Mary's Song of Praise

"My soul magnifies the Lord, and my spirit rejoices in God my Savior,

for he has looked with favor on the lowliness of his servant.

Surely, from now on all generations will call me blessed;

for the Mighty One has done great things for me and holy is his name.

His mercy is for those who fear him from generation to generation."

Preparation

The preceding passage is from the *Magnificat*. It sums up much of what Catholics believe about Mary. "All generations will call me blessed" has been our focus. Mary very clearly, and without fanfare, "magnifies the Lord." Before preparing today's lesson, read the entire Magnificat (Luke 1:46-56) to establish Mary in your heart.

For your class activity, you will need a picture of Mary and Jesus from an old Christmas card or picture book.

Scripture Sharing

Read or discuss the stories about Mary in this leaflet. Tell the stories individually and allow the children to discuss Mary's experience after each one.

Discussion

• Give the children time to do the activity on page one of the leaflet. List the words on the board as the children decode them.

• Ask the children to find examples of when Mary was faithful, brave, helpful, humble, caring, and prayerful in the Bible.

• Give the children time to think about those who love them. Then ask about a time when those people reminded them of Mary.

Faith Journey Activity

Create a silhouette of Mary, either life-size or individual size. Ask the children to fill Mary with her many characteristics. This can be done by using words or images that best represent her. Attach this project under the heading *Mary*.

Answers to Word Scramble: Faithful, Brave, Helpful, Humble, Caring, Prayerful.

• Lesson Eight •
Places in the
Catholic Church

"The Church is, accordingly, a *sheepfold*, the sole and necessary gateway to which is Christ. It is also the flock of which God himself foretold that he would be the shepherd, and whose sheep, even though governed by human shepherds, are unfailingly nourished and led by Christ himself... who gave his life for his sheep...Often, too, the Church is called the *building* of God. The Lord compared himself to the stone which the builders rejected, but which was made into the corner-stone. On this foundation the Church is built...and from it receives solidity and unity" (*Catechism of the Catholic Church*, #754, #756).

Leader Meditation
A reading from Psalm 84:1-4.

Preparation

Visit the church at a time when no formal rites are in progress. Kneel silently before the Lord for a few moments. When you have entered into holiness and silence, pray for the guidance and insight you need to correctly teach the children. Be aware of the different elements of the church: the altar, baptismal font, the tabernacle and sanctuary lamp, the lectern, the Easter candle, the Stations, and the reconciliation room. Meditate on the many ways and times these items touched your life, personally and spiritually.

Prepare a paper with the following list: altar, candles, crucifix, tabernacle, sanctuary lamp, lectern, Easter candle, baptismal font, Stations of the Cross, reconciliation room. Make a copy for each child.

Scripture Sharing

Instead of reading from Scripture, let the children tell their own "prayer stories." Give them time to think about their prayer times. Explain that they are going to be the storytellers today. Then ask for volunteers when someone is ready to share their favorite times and places of prayer. Ask them, especially, to tell about any prayers that were or were not answered.

Discussion

• Read the first paragraph from the leaflet. Then talk about praying in church. After assuring them that prayer is good at any time and any place ask, "Why is the church a special place to pray?"

• Pass out the papers you prepared. If possible, take the children into the church to find and identify each item on the paper. If this is not possible, read the paragraphs mentioning these things from the leaflet. Ask them to take their lists to church the next time they go to Mass and check off each item they find.

• Ask the children if they remember what the priest, deacon, and altar servers were wearing. Then go over these items from the leaflet.

• Give them time to do the *Words to Think About* section of the leaflet.

Faith Journey Activity

Have the children illustrate some item(s) in the church that they remember and write the name of the item beneath the picture. Tape these drawings under the heading *Our Church*.

• Lesson Nine •
Who's Who in
the Church

" 'Among the Christian faithful by divine institution there exists in the Church sacred ministers, who are also called clerics in law, and other Christian faithful who are also called laity.' In both groups there are those Christian faithful who, professing the evangelical counsels, are consecrated to God and so serve the Church's saving mission" (*Catechism of the Catholic Church*, #934).

Leader Meditation

The Call to Service

Lord, you have called me to this special purpose, to make your ways known to the little ones in your flock. Help me to inspire in them a love for your Church, an obedience to your teachings, an understanding of their own call to serve, and a listening ear to those who have been chosen to lead them. Renew my respect for each member of your Church, clergy and lay. Clarify for me the importance of structure and leadership. I ask this in the name of your Son, Jesus, who stands forever as head of your Body, the Church. Amen

Preparation

Copy the match-up lists for the children to use after your discussion.

Member Match-Up

1. Jesus Christ	A. Successors of the Apostles
2. Priests	B. God's workers in the world
3. Laity	C. Members of a religious order
4. Pope	D. Assists priests in caring for the people
5. Deacons	E. The bishops' co-workers
6. Nuns	F. Head of the Church
7. Bishops	G. Successor to Peter

Collect pictures from magazines, newspapers, etc. showing people working with people, helping people.

Scripture Sharing

Read or tell in your own words about the commissioning of the apostles (Matthew 16:13). Encourage discussion of this passage.

Discussion

• Using the leaflets, go over the list of Church members with the children. Allow time for questions and discussion.

• Refer to today's story about building Jesus' Church. Ask the children what promise Jesus was making when he told Peter, "You are Peter (which means rock), and on this rock I will build my church, and the gates of Hades will not prevail against it"?

• Who does Peter's work in the Church today?

• Who are the apostles' successors?

• What is our work in the Church?

• Go over the questions on page two of the leaflet. Since the children may not know the names of the people listed, they will need your help in identifying the particular members.

Faith Journey Activity

Have the children make a collage of the pictures you have brought in. Under the collage write, "We Work for the Church" and place it under the heading *Church People*.

Answers: 1,F; 2,E; 3,B; 4,G; 5,D; 6,C; 7,A

• Lesson Ten • Catholics and Prayer

"It is always possible to pray: The time of the Christian is that of the risen Christ who is with us always, no matter what tempests may arise (cf Mt 28:20; Lk 8:24). Our time is in the hands of God…" (*Catechism of Catholic Church,* #2743).

Leader Meditation

Sit quietly in a comfortable chair. Close your eyes and listen to the sounds around you. Quiet your mind by picturing a favorite spot: on the seashore, by a babbling brook, in a meadow. Allow the sounds around you to enter into your picture. Now place God in the picture with you. What will you say to God? What will God say to you? Wait for your answers. Allow yourself as much time as it takes to complete this image. Slowly return to the sounds of your room. Say a prayer of gratitude to God for sharing this moment with you.

Preparation

Think about times when prayer has been especially important to you. Have you ever gone through a period when prayer seemed impossible? These "dark nights" happen to all of us. Create a special prayer for the next time you feel like you're drifting from God. Tape this prayer in a conspicuous place to use as needed.

For your activity in this lesson, you will need a 3" x 5" index card for each child. Print the child's name on the top line followed by "Special Prayer."

Scripture Sharing

Read or tell in your own words, the passage from Luke 11:1-13. Encourage a discussion of the words in the passage. Do the children truly believe that God answers prayer?

 Discussion

• Give the children time to do the project, *Prayer: A Conversation Between You and God.* When they are finished, invite them to share their answers with the class.

• Ask the children "During Mass, when do we pray together?" The answer, of course, is at all times. Talk about how singing, listening, and just being together with other people in the church are forms of prayer.

• If the children do not already know the Sign of the Cross, help them learn the motions and the meaning behind the sign.

• Ask the children to choose one or two of the prayers in their leaflet. They should say at least one prayer each night this week. If time permits, explain the rosary to them. Although they may not be able to learn it in this short time, it would be good for them to understand the basic concept, the prayers, and the mysteries the rosary represent.

 Faith Journey Activity

Give each child a 3" x 5" index card and ask all of them to write a short, personal prayer. Place each individual prayer into an envelope with the child's name and "My Personal Prayer" written on it.

Add the the prayers under the heading *The Church Prays.*

• Lesson Eleven •
Catholic Practices

"It is clear…that, in the supremely wise arrangement of God, sacred Tradition, Sacred Scripture, and the Magisterium of the Church are so connected and associated that one of them cannot stand without the others. Working together, each in its own way, under the action of the one Holy Spirit, they all contribute effectively to the salvation of souls" (*Catechism of the Catholic Church*, #95 — see also #91–94).

Leader Meditation

Tradition is important to the Catholic Church. Many people leave the church and return later because they miss the tradition and the rituals that bond all Catholics to the ancient Church. Think about your own experiences with Church tradition. If you couldn't attend Church, which traditions would you miss most? Which traditions bind you most closely to God? Which traditions bring you into closest contact with Jesus and his teachings? When do you feel most Catholic in your worship? When do you feel most Christian? Allow yourself some time to meditate on what it means to be Catholic.

Preparation

Collect a fair-sized rock for each child to paint. They will need room to write the word Jesus and one tradition which they will select. Also make cardboard rocks they can illustrate for your *Faith Journey Map*.

Scripture Sharing

Read or tell in your own words, the story of the two foundations found in Luke 6:46-50. Explain that foundation can be many things, for example, rocks, sand, beliefs. Ask them if foundations can crack. How can they be fixed? Discuss what they think is the Church's foundation. How is it different from where they live?

Discussion

• Discuss traditions with the children. Encourage them to share some traditions they have in their own families. Why are these traditions important? Do any of their family traditions go back to the traditions of their grandparents? Have they helped create any new traditions? Ask if these traditions are as important as the older ones and if so, why.

• Read the section *A Year as a Catholic* together. Discuss the ways that Mass is a "remembering" tradition that connects us with God.

• Talk about the Church's current season. What color are the vestments? What does the color mean?

• Read the section *A Dictionary of Catholic Traditions*. Ask which of these traditions will help them become more like Jesus (corporal and spiritual works of mercy)? Which ones are about prayer (contemplation, novena, retreat)? Which ones help us to think about Jesus' love (benediction, genuflection, breviary)? Which ones are about helping us to become stronger spiritually (fast and abstinence)?

• Have the children choose one tradition to write on their rocks. Let them decorate the rocks and use them as reminders of Jesus.

Faith Journey Activity

Have the children either name or illustrate their chosen tradition on the paper "rocks." Under the heading *Catholic Traditions,* print the words "The Church's One Foundation" and add the children's paper rocks.

• Lesson Twelve •
Catholics
and Church

"By reason of their special vocation it belongs to the laity to seek the kingdom of God by engaging in temporal affairs and directing them according to God's will....It pertains to them in a special way so to illuminate and order all temporal things with which they are closely associated that these may always be effected and grow according to Christ and may be the glory of the Creator and Redeemer" (*Catechism of the Catholic Church,* #898 — see also #897–913).

Leader Meditation
A reading from John 14:15-17.

 ## Preparation

The Church founded by Jesus Christ continues through the guidance and workings of the Holy Spirit, who dwells in every member. The children in your care are preparing for their baptism, in the Spirit and truth. To understand the unity and power of the Church, the children must first realize the unity brought about by the Spirit, working through its members. This lesson will dwell on the Spirit within the Church.

For your activity, you will need a start-off list of ideas and projects that the children can do for God and the Church. This should be set in a large cutout of a dove or flame. Also, prepare smaller cutouts for the Faith Journey Activity.

 ## Scripture Sharing

Read or tell in your words the promise of the Holy Spirit, John 14:15-31.

 ## Discussion

• Discuss the presence of the Holy Spirit in all members of the church. Ask what Jesus meant when he said, "I will not leave you orphaned."

• Allow the children time to complete the project, *What Is the Church?* Discuss the unity of the members through the Holy Spirit.

• Talk about ways the Holy Spirit works in the Church: helping the pope and bishops lead and govern the Church, helping priests and deacons guide and teach the people, and helping people spread God's Word and love to the whole world.

• Discuss ways the children can work for God and the Church. Encourage them as a group, to create ideas and projects they can do this week.

 ## Faith Journey Activity

Pass out a dove cutout to each child. Have them print their names on their doves. Ask them to write a prayer to the Holy Spirit to guide them as they too work for the Church. Then tape the doves under the heading, *We Are The Church.* Leave room underneath each dove to write the child's promise for this week.

Ask the children to pick one activity from the list. Have them journal their contributions for a week. Encourage them to recognize the Holy Spirit helping them. They should, if possible, have at least *one* picture of themselves in action. Place their entries with the photograph under the heading, *We are the Church,* at your next gathering.

• Lesson One •
The Sacraments

"Sacraments are 'powers that comes forth' from the Body of Christ, which is ever-living and life-giving. They are actions of the Holy Spirit at work in his Body, the Church. They are 'the masterworks of God' in the new and everlasting covenant" (*The Catechism of the Catholic Church*, #1116).

Leader Meditation
A reading from Matthew 28:16-20.

Preparation

Jesus promises, "I am with you always, to the end of the age." Through the Holy Spirit, he remains active and alive. Through the sacraments, there are "visible signs" of the Lord's presence in the Church and our lives. Each sacrament we receive not only increases the Lord's presence but also increases our own awareness of that presence. Jesus becomes, in a very real way, a part of each spiritual milestone in our life. We don't walk our journey of faith alone — Jesus walks with us every step of the way. Your headings for this section include: The Journey; Baptism; Confirmation; Eucharist; Penance; Anointing of the Sick; Marriage; Holy Orders; Old Testament; New Testament; Early Church; Christian Living; Social Justice; God's Greatest Gift; Life.

Stepping Stones on the Journey. Remove the children's work from the journey map. Staple each child's work together with a cover sheet, making a book of their Inquiry as a keepsake. Beneath the remaining words now left on the map, add seven large stones, cut from brown construction paper. Title each stone with a different sacrament name. Explain to the children that, at their baptism, Jesus joins them on their journey and remains with them through the sacraments. Cut out girl and boy figures, one for each child in your group, to use during the journey. Leave the faces and clothing for the children to add during their activity time. This is one option.

If you choose to do the second activity (see paragraph two under Faith Journey Activity), you will need pictures/images of the children and Jesus, stones large enough for a child's foot, cutouts of the shape of Jesus' foot, and representations of the sacraments.

Scripture Sharing

Read or tell in your own words the story of Jesus' birth, Luke 2:1-20. Encourage the children to talk about what Jesus' birth means to them. Then explain that Jesus came to be with them forever. They're about to learn all the special ways Jesus will be a part of their lives.

Discussion

• After reviewing the section *How Do You Say, 'I Love You'?*, start a discussion of ways to express love for family and friends. Write their answers on the board for later use.

• Move on to the section *How Does Jesus Say, 'I Love You'?* Let the children read over this. Each child should read the ways Jesus said "I love you" when he was in the world. Then discuss the similarities/differences between their expressions and those of Jesus.

• Explain to the children that the sacraments are Jesus' way of loving and being with us during all the important times of our lives. It's important that they understand Jesus is always with us. Through the sacraments, Jesus celebrates with us as we grow in the faith.

Faith Journey Activity

Create a garden of kids, with Jesus in the middle. Use illustrations or actual pictures of your children. This will allow them to visualize the end. Let them help you place the stepping stones along the journey. Let them finish the figures of themselves and place these at the beginning of the stepping stones. Or, place real stones in a row leading to an image of Jesus. Each stone should be parallel to a sacrament. Cut out some footprints of Jesus so they can "see" his presence with them. As they pass a sacrament, allow the child to step on/remove/or advance a stone from or to a garden. Distribute the books you prepared with their Inquiry activities. Don't forget to add the previous week's journal entries and pictures to your *Faith Journey Map*.

· Lesson Two · The Sacrament of Baptism

"The faith required for Baptism is not a perfect and mature faith, but a beginning that is called to develop. The catechumen or the godparent is asked: 'What do you ask of God's Church?' The response is: 'Faith'" (*Catechism of the Catholic Church*, #1253, see also #1246–1249).

Leader Meditation

A reading from Mark 1:4-5, 7-8.

Most of us can't recall our own baptisms. Yet many times along our journey, we review and remake the promises made for us. In preparation for this lesson, renew your promises, dwelling on each of them. Consider how well you have lived in the spirit of that sacrament.

 ## Preparation

You will need a baby doll, a small bowl of water, oil, a white dress for the doll, and a candle. If you don't have one, ask your pastor or deacon for a copy of the rite of baptism. You will be using this during your discussion time. For the activity section, you will need white paper, crayons or markers, and scissors. You might want to find or make stencils of the following symbols: water, oil, white garment, candle.

 ## Scripture Sharing

Read or tell in your own words the story of John the Baptist, Mark 1:1-8. Discuss the children's thoughts on what John meant by being baptized in the Holy Spirit. After allowing time for questions, read the baptism of Jesus, Mark 1:9-11. Encourage a discussion about the difference between Jesus' baptism and the baptisms of the others in the Jordan River. Emphasize God's participation in the baptism of Jesus — and God's participation in their own baptisms.

 ## Discussion

• Begin with a discussion of the children's place in their families. What does belonging to a family mean? What responsibilities do they have to the family? How do they show their families that they love them?

• Read the section, *Joining the Family of God*. Discuss this new family they will be joining, the similarities and differences. Relate the discussion of their own family responsibilities to those of the family of God. What and how will they give? What and how will they receive?

• Read together the section *The Signs of Baptism* from the handout. Discuss, at length, each symbol and its meaning to them.

• Using the baby doll, water, oil, white dress, and candle, go through the rite of baptism with the children. Ask two children to be godparents. If the children are receptive, repeat the baptism, allowing others to be the minister and godparents.

 ## Faith Journey Activity

Ask the children to think about the symbols used in the sacrament of baptism. Then give them time to illustrate one symbol each and cut it out. If you only have one or two children in your group, they can each create two symbols. Tape their symbols under the stepping stone labeled *Baptism*. Write, "We are welcomed in God's family."

Or, since each child in the class is a member of a family, ask them to list their family responsibilities. Then, make a separate list of their responsibilities to the family of God. How will they fulfill these duties? On their lists, they should answer that question.

· Lesson Three · The Sacrament of Confirmation

"It must be explained to the faithful that the reception of the sacrament of Confirmation is necessary for the completion of baptismal grace. For 'by the sacrament of Confirmation, [the baptized] are more perfectly bound to the Church and are enriched with a special strength of the Holy Spirit. Hence they are, as true witnesses of Christ, more strictly obliged to spread and defend the faith by word and deed'" (*Catechism of the Catholic Church,* #1285, see also #1286–1314).

Leader Meditation
A reading from Acts 1:8-11.

We have all been witnesses to the fulfillment of Jesus' promise to send the Holy Spirit. This Spirit comes, also as promised, with the power to make us witnesses "to the ends of the earth." Your witness is your most effective tool in passing on the faith to the children in your care. Now and before each lesson, say the following excerpt from the Prayer to the Holy Spirit: *"O God, you have instructed the hearts of the faithful by the light of the Holy Spirit. Grant that through the same Holy Spirit we may always be truly wise and rejoice in the Spirit's consolation. Through Christ our Lord."*

 Preparation

Prepare two or three gift boxes for each child to decorate. Cut these out of brightly colored construction paper. Cut three to four slips of paper per child.

 Scripture Sharing

Before you begin your *Scripture Sharing,* ask the children to pretend they are the disciples. Jesus has just gone to heaven with the promise to send the Holy Spirit. They have come together to talk about what Jesus meant. Now ask the children to listen to the story in Acts 2:1-13 and pretend it is happening to them.

 Discussion

• Ask, "What happened to you when you were together in that room?" "Did you feel frightened, amazed, confused?" Explain that the disciples felt all these things. But after the Holy Spirit filled their hearts, they understood everything and spoke about Jesus bravely.

• Explain that confirmation will help them to understand God's love. It's like growing up in the Spirit. Talk about growing up. Ask how they answered the question about the things they can do this year that they couldn't do last year. They are stronger and braver.

• Carry this discussion over to explain how confirmation helps them to grow up in the Spirit, to use their talents for God's Church. Ask them to name gifts and talents they can use to help the Church. Write these things on the board.

• Read the section, *What Will Happen at Your Confirmation?* Discuss the celebration and their choice of a sponsor and a confirmation name.

 Faith Journey Activity

Discuss the gifts and talents the children have to offer to God's Church. Give them their gift boxes to decorate. Tell them to make a gift tag to the Spirit. Give them a few slips describing their special gifts. Make sure these gifts aren't tangible. Attach these slips to each box and clip or tape these boxes under the heading *Confirmation*. Write, "Our special gifts to the Spirit."

· Lesson Four ·
The Eucharist

"The holy Eucharist completes Christian initiation. Those who have been raised to the dignity of the royal priesthood by Baptism and configured more deeply to Christ by Confirmation participate with the whole community in the Lord's own sacrifice by means of the Eucharist" (*Catechism of the Catholic Church,* #1322, see also #1323–1381).

Leader Meditation

A reading from John 6:47-51.

As Catholics, our faith in the Real Presence of our Lord in the Eucharist sets us apart from many other Christian churches. Before you can pass on this faith to the children, meditate on the passage, John 6:22-66. This is the central Catholic truth upon which all Catholic truths are based. Preparing the children to know, understand, and believe takes a faith equal to that of the apostles, who answered Jesus, saying, "Lord, to whom can we go? You have the words of eternal life."

 Preparation

For your *Scripture Sharing,* bring a loaf of bread and a bottle of grape juice.

For your activity, you will need to cut out one paper host and chalice for each child. Cut out several pictures representing the Resurrection of Jesus.

 Scripture Sharing

Read *The Last Supper of Jesus* from the first page of the children's leaflets or read a Scripture passage on the institution of the Eucharist: Mark 14:22-25, Matthew 26:26-29, or Luke 22:14-23. Share the bread and grape juice with them as you tell the story. Explain that you are only "acting out" the story now, but when they receive holy Communion, they will be receiving the Lord in truth.

 Discussion

• Encourage the children to talk about special meals they share with their families. Meal times are special times for families to be together and celebrate. For that reason, Jesus chose the simple elements of bread and wine to be with his people for all time.

• Read the section *The Real Presence* to the children. Encourage them to discuss their feelings about this sacrament.

• Read or ask a child to read the section *The Promise.* Ask the children why the people found this saying "too hard to believe." Do they find it hard to believe? Why or why not? Discuss what they learned about their faith during their Inquiry sessions. Explain the importance of believing in this mystery and in Jesus' promise that "Whoever eats this bread will live forever." Allow plenty of time for this discussion.

 Faith Journey Activity

Read *A Super Kind of Love* together. Give each child a host to decorate in honor of Jesus' super love. Add them to their chalice. Tape their chalices to the map under the heading *Eucharist.* Write, "Jesus brings God's love to us in holy Communion."

• Lesson Five •
The Sacrament of Penance

"'Those who approach the sacrament of Penance obtain pardon from God's mercy for the offense committed against [God], and are, at the same time, reconciled with the Church which they have wounded by their sins and which by charity, by example, and by prayer labors for their conversion'" (*Catechism of the Catholic Church*, #1422, see also #1423–1445).

Leader Meditation
A reading from Luke 15:11-32.

Read the entire passage from the Gospel of Luke three times. The first time, put yourself in the place of the father. Feel the father's feelings. Respond with the father's reactions. Do the same with the older son, and finally with the younger son. Consider how many times you have been placed in similar positions, felt similar feelings, responded with similar responses. We have all been there. These experiences will also be familiar to the children.

 ## Preparation

For your activity, you will need one sheet of 8" x 11" white (or light colored) construction paper for each child. Cut the paper into bookmark-sized strips, 2 1/8" x 8 1/2". Read the instructions for the activity and make up a sample bookmark for them to follow.

 ## Scripture Sharing

Depending upon the ages of your children, read *The Boy Who Ran Away* from the leaflet or the gospel passage telling the story of the Prodigal Son. Choose children to imagine they are the father and the younger son. Encourage them to share their feelings.

Discussion

• Read Nicholas' story on page one of the leaflet. After the children answered the questions, discuss their responses. Why was it important for Nicholas to say, "I'm sorry"; for Colin to say, "I forgive you"?

• Encourage a discussion about times when the children did something for which they were sorry. Were they forgiven? How did it feel to be (or not be) forgiven?

• Move the discussion to times the children were angry at someone else. Were they forgiving? How did it feel to forgive (or not to forgive)?

 ## Faith Journey Activity

Pass out the construction paper bookmarks. On one side, ask them to write, "I'm sorry." They can decorate this appropriately. On the backside, ask them to write a generic prayer of forgiveness. Let them keep this project, if they want. If possible, laminate the bookmarks. They should be encouraged to keep them in their Bibles, and use them anytime they seek forgiveness. If they want to display them, attach the actual bookmarks or copies under the heading *Penance*.

• Lesson Six •
The Sacrament of the Anointing of the Sick

"'By the sacred anointing of the sick and the prayer of the priests the whole Church commends those who are ill to the suffering and glorified Lord, that he may raise them up and save them. And indeed she exhorts them to contribute to the good of the People of God by freely uniting themselves to the Passion and death of Christ.' This sacred anointing of the sick was instituted by Christ our Lord as a true and proper sacrament of the New Testament. It is alluded to indeed by Mark, but is recommended to the faithful and promulgated by James the apostle and brother of the Lord" (*Catechism of the Catholic Church*, #1499, #1511, see also #1499–1532).

Leader Meditation
A reading from James 5:14-16.

Preparation

Prepare an 8 ½" x 11" sheet of poster board or cardboard for each child. On the top of the card, print the words, "Jesus Sends His Healing and His Love." Collect pictures illustrating this truth: people in the hospital, in wheelchairs, elder people, children playing, families praying together, a family around a sick bed, nurses, doctors, etc. Try to find pictures in which the people are smiling.

 ## Scripture Sharing

Read or tell in your own words the Scripture passage John 2:1. Remind the children about their last lesson — that Jesus forgives our sins. By forgiving our sins, Jesus heals the wound in our soul. When Jesus told the man his sins were forgiven, the people didn't believe. But when he told the man to stand up and go home, they believed. Why was it easier for them to believe he could heal the body than the soul?

 ## Discussion

• Read *Jenny's Grandma* to the children. Ask why Jenny was upset with the priest. The priest said he was telling the truth, that Grandma would get better "in God's way." What did he mean? What are the three promises that came true?

• Discuss and illustrate the four steps to healing on page one of the children's leaflets. You can emphasize these steps by acting them out or letting the children act them out.

• Talk about the four ways God can heal. Take each topic, one at a time. It's important for the children to understand that, while Jesus has the power to heal, sometimes Jesus helps the sick person in different ways.

• Encourage the children to talk about times when someone they love was sick or died. Allow plenty of time for this. Help them understand that even death can lead to happiness — in heaven with God.

 ## Faith Journey Activity

Have the children make their "Jesus Sends…" cards for someone they know — a neighbor, relative,… Let them choose from the pictures you collected to illustrate their cards. Make copies for your *Faith Journey Map* and return the cards at the end of the session. Attach the copies under the heading *Anointing of the Sick*.

· Lesson Seven ·
The Sacrament of Marriage

"'The matrimonial covenant, by which a man and a woman establish between themselves a partnership of the whole of life, is by its nature ordered toward the good of the spouses and the procreation and education of offspring; this covenant between baptized persons has been raised by Christ the Lord to the dignity of a sacrament'" (#1601, see also #1602–1664).

Leader Meditation
A reading from Mark 10:6-8.

After meditating on the above Scripture, think about your feelings about the passage. Consider couples you know who are having difficulties in their marriages. Consider, also, the difficulties you may have encountered in relationships. Do you believe the Scripture above can help in these situations? If so, how? If not, can you think of a passage that will help? (Try Matthew 11:28. Your own spiritual preparation is vital in this lesson.)

 ## Preparation

You will need two 8 ½" x 11" pieces of different colored construction paper per child. Create a frame, using the two sheets, with the darker color as the frame. Make sure you have some magazines avail-able for the children to use. Cut out a man and a woman for each child. You will also need extra child figures to add brothers and sisters to their *Faith Journey Map*.

 ## Scripture Sharing

Read or tell in your own words the passage on marriage from Mark 10:6-8. Encourage the children to discuss their feelings about marriage and family. Keep in mind that some may come from broken families or have friends or family members who have experienced divorce. If the situation seems to call for it, assure the children that God loves all families, even though some may no longer live together. Don't rush this time of sharing.

Discussion

• The *Catechism of the Catholic Church* states, "No one is without a family in this world: the Church is a home and family for everyone, especially those who 'labor and are heavy laden'" (#1658). Discuss this teaching with the children.

• Read *Three to Get Married* from the children's leaflet. Discuss ways God helps people who are married. Explain that marriage is not only for the bride and groom but for all their children for all time.

• Encourage them to talk about their families, especially about how families help one another in times of need.

• Read *Married Forever*. Discuss what the ideas conveyed regarding divorce. Ask the children about the possibility of remarriage. How should it be handled? After a time of sharing, read the section on annulments.

• Return to the subject of family. Explain that there are many kinds of family — some with parents living together or separately, some with other members of the family serving as caretakers, some with foster parents. Explain that God is always a partner in every family.

 Faith Journey Activity

Ask the children to find images of marriage. The children should be allowed to use images from the magazines to create their work. Then, tape these frames under the *Marriage* heading. Give the children their frames and ask them to glue the different images of marriage to the frame. This should be a collage of marriages, not simply weddings.

· Lesson Eight · The Sacrament of Holy Orders

"Holy Orders is the sacrament through which the mission entrusted by Christ to his apostles continues to be exercised in the Church until the end of time: thus it is the sacrament of apostolic ministry. It includes three degrees: episcopate, presbyterate, and diaconate" (*Catechism of the Catholic Church*, #1536; see also #1536–1600).

Leader Meditation
A reading from Hebrews 5:1-6.

 Preparation

The children will be drawing freehand for their activity this week. You will need drawing paper, markers, or crayons. It might help to have pictures of a bishop, a priest, and a deacon for them to copy.

 Scripture Sharing

Read or tell in your own words the Scripture passage from John 13:1-16 about the washing of the apostles' feet. Ask the children if they know what Jesus was trying to tell his apostles. He was commanding them to serve God by serving others.

 Discussion

• Who are the successors of the apostles today? How does the pope serve God by serving others? The bishops? Your parish priest? Your deacon? Give plenty of time to this portion of your discussion.

• Ask the children to read about the works of the priest from page one of the leaflet. After they have finished, discuss how each of these services is performed in your own church.

• On the board, write the names of your bishop, pastor, assistant priests, and deacon. Go over the differences between the three levels of orders together.

• Ask questions based on the delegated responsibilities of each ordained person. For example, "If your uncle wants to become a priest, who can ordain him?" "Who can hear your confession?" Have the children fill out the answers to the questions, using the names listed on the board. They can answer these questions using the ordained members of your parish or by naming the position.

• Ask if any of the children would like to be called to serve God in this special way — and why do they think they would like it. Encourage the girls to answer as well as the boys.

 ## Faith Journey Activity

Have the children draw a picture of a bishop, priest, or deacon using one of the services they are ordained to perform. Tape their drawings under the heading *Holy Orders*. Add the words, "Called to serve God's people."

• Lesson Nine •
The People of God

"From the beginning until 'the fullness of time,' the joint mission of the Father's Word and Spirit remains *hidden*, but it is at work. God's Spirit prepares for the time of the Messiah. Neither is fully revealed but both are already promised, to be watched for and welcomed at their manifestation. So, for this reason, when the Church reads the Old Testament, she searches there for what the Spirit, 'who has spoken through the prophets,' wants to tell us about Christ" (*Catechism of the Catholic Church*, #702).

Leader Meditation

Read and meditate upon one or more of the following passages: Genesis, chapters 15-21, 24-46; Exodus, chapters 7-16. Throughout the Old Testament, we see God's ever-constant presence with and for the protection of the people. We also see the people's constant battle with their own faith and fears. After you read the chapters of your choice, review your life. Identify those times when you knew God's presence and those times when you felt abandoned by God. Allow this to merge with the Scripture passage. What does it tell you about God? What does it tell you about yourself and your faith?

 ## Preparation

You will be taking down the Sacrament section of your *Faith Journey Map* and replacing it with *How the Church Grew*. Your map will now have four sections: Old Testament, New Testament, Early Church, and Today's Church.

For this lesson, you will need to find or make figures from Old Testament stories: Abraham, Isaac, Moses, and David.

 ## Scripture Sharing

Read or tell in your own words the anointing of David, 1 Samuel 16:1-13. Explain that David was chosen by God to lead the people. The promised Messiah would come from the line of David.

Discussion

• Read the Old Testament stories from the children's leaflet. Discuss God's role in all the stories they heard. Do they believe that God still watches over and protects the people in the Church?

• Encourage the children to talk about God's presence in their lives. When do they pray? Do they believe God hears their prayer?

• For many years, God promised to send a Savior. The people told the stories over and over, passing them down from each generation. Share stories about your grandparents that were passed down through the family. Encourage the class to share, too.

• Every Hebrew child waited and hoped the Messiah would come in his or her lifetime. But God waited, which tested their faith repeatedly before the Messiah came. Ask the children if they know who was the promised Messiah or Savior. Question what made him so special that he was called the "Messiah" or "Savior."

• Jesus makes our life in the Church different from the children of the Old Testament. Ask how the children's lives are different because Jesus has come. How would their lives be different if he hadn't come? Ask these questions of yourself, too.

 Faith Journey Activity

Let each child choose one Old Testament figure. Ask them to tell you something about the figure they chose. They can write a story or color (if a cutout is used). For the older children, ask them to find a description of their figure and create him/her by using pieces of images. Attach and label them under the heading *Old Testament*. This should be an identifiable collage of images.

• Lesson Ten • Who Is Jesus Christ?

"As Lord, Christ is also head of the Church, which is his Body. Taken up to heaven and glorified after he had thus fully accomplished his mission, Christ dwells on earth in his Church. The redemption is the source of the authority that Christ, by virtue of the Holy Spirit, exercises over the Church. 'The kingdom of Christ [is] already present in mystery,' 'on earth, the seed and the beginning of the kingdom'" (*Catechism of the Catholic Church*, #669, see also #541, #792, #1088).

Leader Meditation
A reading from John 15:1-5.

 Preparation

Make "branches" from thin florist's wire. Add leaves cut from green construction paper. You will need at least six leaves per child. Make another branch for yourself to add names of people active in your parish — priest, deacon, religious education teachers, altar servers, etc.

 Scripture Sharing

Read or tell in your own words the Good Shepherd passage, John 10:1-16. Encourage a discussion on the meaning of Jesus' words: "I am the good shepherd. I know my own and my own know me." Who does Jesus call his "own"?

 Discussion

• Discuss the quotes on page one of the children's leaflet. Read them one at a time and ask the children what the quote tells us about Jesus. What does it tell us about God the Father? What does it tell us about ourselves and our Church? Encourage different interpretations as long as they don't contradict truth.

• Allow the children time to do the exercises on page two of the leaflet. When they have finished, encourage them to share their answers.

• Ask the children if they can tell the stories referred to in the section, *The Miracles of Jesus.* If they are unfamiliar with a story, help them find it in the Bible. If they are old enough, have them read it aloud. Otherwise, read it to them yourself. What does each story tell us about Jesus? About God's love?

Faith Journey Activity

Place all the "branches" you prepared in the center of your activity table. Use the branches to create a "vine" beneath the words "Jesus is the vine; we are the branches." This whole section will go under the heading *New Testament.*

Jesus described himself in many ways. See how many you can name. Use actual props or images to depict some of the ways Jesus described himself (ie, bread, light, vine...). Place a card next to each prop/image. The card should have the book and chapter listed as reference. The descriptions should then be written on the leaves which will be taped to the branches on the map.

• Lesson Eleven •
The Early Church

"Jesus is the Father's Emissary. From the beginning of his ministry, he 'called to him those whom he desired;.... And he appointed twelve, whom also he name apostles, to be with him, and to be sent out to preach.' From then on, they would also be his 'emissaries' (Greek *apostoloi*). In them, Christ continues his own mission: 'As the Father has sent me, even so I send you.' The apostles' ministry is the continuation of his mission; Jesus said to the Twelve: 'he who receives you receives me'" (*Catechism of the Catholic Church,* #858, see also #425, #551, #1086).

Leader Meditation
A reading from Romans 12:9-13.

After meditating on the Scripture passage, consider your parish and the ways in which these marks of a true Christian are apparent — or missing. What can you do to emphasize these attributes among your brother and sister parishioners?

Preparation

For today's activity, you will need a sheet of paper, a pencil, markers or crayons. You will also need a lot of time.

Scripture Sharing

Read or tell in your own words the passage on the Mission of the Twelve Apostles, Matthew 10:5-15. Discuss ways that the Church still carries on this mission. Point out especially Jesus' instructions that they are to "go to the lost sheep"; to "proclaim the good news"; to "cure the sick..."; and to "give without payment."

Discussion

• Read or have the children read, *Jesus Makes a Promise* from the first page of the leaflet. Ask them if they know who Jesus meant by "the Spirit of truth."

• Allow the children time to answer the questions. When they have finished, encourage them to share their answers with the class.

• Read *The Birthday of the Church* together. Discuss ways that the Holy Spirit still guides and leads the Church today. Ask them if they can tell you special times when the Holy Spirit will come to them.

• Read *A Man Named Saul.* Discuss the changes in Paul after Jesus came to him. Ask the children to think of some changes that have already happened for them through prayer and study. How can these changes shape their lives?

 ## Faith Journey Activity

Have the children choose one of the stories they heard in this lesson to illustrate. If you have brought in a children's Bible, show them where they can find their chosen stories. Have them label their stories, "Jesus Makes a Promise"; "The Apostles Receive the Spirit"; "Saul Becomes Paul"; etc. Tape or tack these illustrations under the words *Early Church.*

Or create a story based on "Jesus Makes a Promise"; "The Apostles Receive the Spirit"; "Saul Becomes Paul"; etc. and set it in modern times. Encourage the children to incorporate current events. How have the things that are happening in the world affected them? How do they think God would handle the situation? Tape or tack these stories under the heading *Early Church.*

• Lesson Twelve • The History of the Church

"So that she can fulfill her mission, the Holy Spirit 'bestows upon [the Church] varied hierarchic and charismatic gifts, and in this way directs her.' 'Henceforward the Church, endowed with the gifts of her founder and faithfully observing his precepts of charity, humility and self-denial, receives the mission of proclaiming and establishing among all peoples the Kingdom of Christ and of God, and she is on earth the seed and the beginning of that kingdom'" (*Catechism of the Catholic Church*, #768; see also #541, #731, #767, #849).

Leader Meditation

A reading from Matthew 28:16-20.

With the words from Matthew, Jesus breathed life into his Church. The same words still hold us together today, giving life to the Church, "I am with you always, to the end of the age." Hear Jesus saying them to you always, a constant blessing to you in your ministry to the children.

 ## Preparation

Today's lesson will depend very much on information only you can share. You will need to know and be able to identify the following people for the children: your pastor, deacon, acolytes, lecters, and eucharistic ministers. Also, learn about the name-saints of the children.

For your activity, bring in pictures illustrating the Church throughout history. You can use holy cards with saint pictures, magazine illustrations of the pope, pictures of parishes at Mass, etc. Collect enough pictures to create a collage for your map.

 ## Scripture Sharing

Read Colossians 3:12-17. Ask the children, "How many of the things mentioned in the reading can you find in your parish community today?" (Compassion, kindness, humility, meekness, patience, forgiveness, and love.)

Discussion

• Read *The History of Your Church Family.* Do the children know anything about their name-saints? Encourage a discussion about ways they can learn from the saints, especially those for whom they are named. Do they know the name-saint of their parish? Talk about the special characteristics and charisms of the parish saint.

• Discuss religious communities in your area. How does each community serve God and the Church — missionaries, teachers, those who work in hospitals, those who serve the poor?

• Read *Family Separations.* Discuss other Christian Churches similar to Catholicism. What will be different for the children as Catholic Christians? What will stay the same?

• Several changes occurred because of Vatican II. Take some time to discuss these changes and have the children answer the questions under *The Church Today.* Read *Your Family Story* to the children. Encourage a discussion about family histories and traditions.

 Faith Journey Activity

Assign a saint to each child. Make sure they are easily recognized. Ask the child to make a collage of the traits that made each child's saint special. Have the others guess the saint. Display these in the room. Then print the words, "I am with you always," and attach the collages under the heading *Today's Church.*

• Lesson Thirteen •
Christian
Moral Living

"Since they express [our] fundamental duties towards God and towards [our] neighbor, the Ten Commandments reveal, in their primordial content, *grave* obligations. They are fundamentally immutable, and they oblige always and everywhere. No one can dispense from them. The Ten Commandments are engraved by God in the human heart" (*Catechism of the Catholic Church,* #2072; see also #2052–2082).

Leader Meditation
A reading from Matthew 22:34-40.

 Preparation

Using the commandments, as worded on page two of the leaflet, cut a strip of paper for each commandment (numbers nine and ten are combined). Print the commandments on the strips, leaving room below to give examples. Prepare nine more strips that contain Jesus' "greatest commandments," three with the first and six with the second.

 Scripture Sharing

Read the passage chosen as your own meditation today, Matthew 22:34-40. Explain to the children that Jesus says as long as we obey the two Great Commandments, we will never break the Ten Commandments. Ask them if they can give you examples of obeying the two Great Commandments.

 Discussion

• Discuss the commandments, one at a time, using examples of how they are sometimes kept or broken. Ask which commandment is the hardest to keep.

• Talk about conscience. Ask, "How do you feel when you know you have been unloving?" Discuss their answers to the first question on page two.

• Discuss some of the laws and rules the children live by in their everyday life — family and classroom rules, game rules, traffic rules, etc. How do we help ourselves and others by obeying these laws? What would happen if we had no laws or rules?

• The Ten Commandments are God's way of helping us to love one another. Reiterate the fact that the two Great Commandments help us to follow each of the Ten Commandments.

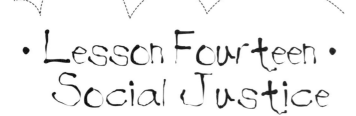 Faith Journey Activity

On the commandment slips, ask the children to give examples of how they can keep the Ten Commandments. Each one should be preceded by one or both of the two Great Commandments. Once these are finished, tape them under the heading *Christian Living.*

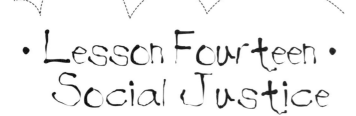

• Lesson Fourteen • Social Justice

"The Church makes a moral judgement about economic and social matters, 'when the fundamental rights of the person or the salvation of souls requires it.' In the moral order she bears a mission distinct from that of political authorities: the Church is concerned with the temporal aspects of the common good because they are ordered to the sovereign Good, our ultimate end. She strives to inspire right attitudes with respect to earthly goods and in socio-economic relationships" (*Catechism of the Catholic Church,* #2420; see also #2408–2463).

Leader Meditation
A reading from Luke 4:18-21.

Preparation

In the children's leaflets, five areas of social concern are listed. Find pictures depicting each area to bring in. You will also need an 8 ¹/₂" x 11" sheet of white construction paper for the children to mount the pictures. If there are parishioners active in any of the areas mentioned, invite them in to discuss the topic(s) with the children. Make sure the topics are age appropriate.

Scripture Sharing

Read the story of Lazarus and the Rich Man from the children's leaflet, or from a children's Bible, Luke 16:19-25. Discuss what the rich man could have done for Lazarus while they were both still alive. Ask why the rich man ignored Lazarus.

Discussion

• Read the entire leaflet together, stopping to discuss ways that the Church helps people who are suffering in the world.

• Discuss what Jesus meant when he said, "Whoever wishes to be great among you must be your servant, and whoever wishes to be first among you must be your slave."

• What are some things the children can do to "be great" in Jesus' eyes. These don't have to be big projects. Suggest things such as sharing with one another, helping smaller children on the playground, doing chores cheerfully at home.

• Help the class to come up with a project (collect food for the poor, make cards for shut-ins, visit the sick, etc.). Begin this project next week and continue it throughout the rest of the catechumenate period.

Faith Journey Activity

Print the words, "Our Church Cares" under the heading *Social Justice.* Have the children mount the pictures you have brought in on the construction paper and label each one.

Ask the children how they can help with some of today's social issues.

Encourage the children to think ahead. What will they tell their kids about what is happening now? Add these to your map.

• Lesson Fifteen •
Life: The Greatest Gift

"Human life is sacred because from its beginning it involves the creative action of God and it remains forever in a special relationship with the Creator, who is its sole end. God alone is the Lord of life from its beginning until its end: no one can under any circumstance claim...the right directly to destroy an innocent human being" (*Catechism of the Catholic Church*, #2258; see also #2259–2330).

Leader Meditation
A reading from Genesis 4:8-11.

 Preparation

You will need four sheets of 8 ¹/₂" x 11" heavy white paper. Draw giant letters L, I, F, E, one on each paper. If you have more than four children, you can make two of each letter to be certain every child has a chance to decorate a letter. You will also need markers, star stickers, glitter glue, magazines, and writing paper.

 Scripture Sharing

Read Matthew 5:21-25 to the children. Discuss why Jesus does not want us to be angry at one another. What has anger to do with killing?

Discussion

• Read the creation story from Genesis to the children. If possible, use a children's Bible with pictures that emphasize God's wondrous gifts to us.

• Encourage the children to talk about things they have made — models, drawings, etc. Ask them to think about how they would feel if someone came along and destroyed what they made. Relate this to God's message on the sacredness of life.

• Read the section on abortion and discuss alternatives to abortion, such as adoption or offering help to a mother who is too poor to feed another child.

• Read the section *Poverty and Hunger* aloud. Then allow the children time to answer the questions on page two. When they have finished, discuss their answers.

• Begin the project you planned during the last session.

• Discuss war. How do wars get started? Relate war to fights and arguments within the family or on the playground. Why do people fight? What can we do to help keep peace in our family or at school?

Faith Journey Activity

Print the words, "God's Greatest Gift" on your map. Let the children decorate and cut out the giant letters L, I, F, E. Make them large enough to incorporate images of life from the magazines. Or, the students can create life appreciation prayers, speaking to the sacredness of life and ways to help preserve it. The prayers should fit into the letters. Tape your activity under the heading *God's Greatest Gift*.

• Lesson Sixteen •
The Dignity of Life

"*Justice* is the moral virtue that consists in the constant and firm will to give their due to God and neighbor. Justice toward God is called the 'virtue of religion.' Justice toward [all] disposes one to respect the rights of each and to establish in human relationships the harmony that promotes equity with regard to persons and to the common good. The just [person], often mentioned in the Sacred Scriptures, is distinguished by habitual right thinking for the uprightness of [one's] conduct toward [one's] neighbor. 'You shall not be partial to the poor or defer to the great, but in righteousness shall judge your neighbor'" (*Catechism of the Catholic Church*, #1807).

Leader Meditation
A reading from Matthew 5:21-26, 43-48.

Preparation

Cut out pictures of God's gifts, and images that aren't gifts, from magazines or old greeting cards. Be certain to include photos of children of different ethnic backgrounds, along with pictures of animals and plant life. You will need tape to create a collage with these pictures. Be sure you have enough pictures to completely fill this section of your *Faith Journey Map*.

Scripture Sharing

Read or tell in your own words the parable of "The Good Samaritan," Luke 10:29-37. Discuss ways the children can be good Samaritans to others, and people who have been good Samaritans to them.

Discussion

• Read the section on prejudice to the children. Ask them if they can give any examples of prejudice in their neighborhoods, their classrooms, or on the playground. The leaflet discusses prejudice as a sin. Ask why this is so.

• Ask the children if any of them have ever been left out of something because of prejudice or discrimination. How did it make them feel? Give examples of people in your community who are being discriminated against. How does God feel about discrimination? Which of Jesus' two Great Commandments are being broken by discrimination and prejudice? (Actually both, since discrimination sins against God and against our neighbor.)

• Read the section *God's World is in Our Hands.* Discuss ways that the children can work to protect God's creation (feeding the birds, planting a garden, etc.).

• Allow the children time to answer the questions about God's gifts, on page two of the leaflets. List the gifts on the board, then talk about ways they can care for God's gifts.

• Plan a garden project. Tell the children you will bring planters to the next session. Ask them to bring in seeds or small plants. Since Lent is coming, set the Easter Vigil as a time for them to take their plants home.

Faith Journey Activity

Have the children select pictures that fit under the heading, *We Care for God's World,* from the posterboard. The images which don't show us caring for the world should be mixed throughout the collage. Have them identify those images and generate a discussion or a list of how we can preserve/care for those things to make them a gift from God. For example, an image of kids littering in the park can be changed by starting a group of volunteers who help keep the park clean.

• Lesson One •
What Is Lent?

"In the liturgy of the Church, it is principally his own Paschal mystery that Christ signifies and makes present. During his earthly life Jesus announced his paschal mystery by his teaching and anticipated it by his actions. When his Hour comes, he lives out the unique event of history which does not pass away; Jesus dies, is buried, rises from the dead, and is seated at the right hand of the Father 'once and for all.' His Paschal mystery is a real event that occurred in our history, but it is unique: all other historical events happen once, and then pass away, swallowed up in the past. The Paschal mystery of Christ, by contrast, cannot remain only in the past, because by his death he destroyed death, and all that Christ is — all that he did and suffered for all — participates in the divine eternity, and so transcends all times while being made present in them all. The event of the Cross and Resurrection *abides* and draws everything toward life" (*Catechism of the Catholic Church*, #1085, see also #1084–1090).

Leader Meditation
A reading from Matthew 16:21-23.

 **Preparation**

Take down the children's work from the catechumenate sessions and staple them into booklets. Title the booklets, "We Learn About Jesus." Prepare your map for a Lenten Journey with eight sections: Lent Begins; Choosing Jesus; Love Cannot Sin; The Creed; The Way of the Cross; The Lord's Prayer; Holy Week; and A New Journey.

Prepare scripts using the temptation dialogue between Jesus and Satan. Set up a portion of the room to represent the wilderness. Allow time in your *Scripture Sharing* so each child has a chance to play a part. For the activity, bring in the following items: Lenten cards with images of Jesus, purple construction paper, crosses made with craft sticks, glue, and ashes and palm branches.

 Scripture Sharing

The story of Jesus' temptation in the wilderness is the basis for today's *Scripture Sharing*. Read the passage once, then invite the children to take turns acting out the dialogue. Follow up with a discussion about how it felt to be tempted (or to be the tempter).

 Discussion

• Read the section, *Three Ways to Resist Temptation*. Tell stories, either personal or fictional, of people being tempted. Encourage the children to discuss ways they would resist the temptation in each story.

• Allow time for the children to list three things they can do during Lent to bring them closer to Jesus. Discuss their answers.

• Discuss the symbols of Lent. What, if anything, do ashes mean to them in everyday life; the color purple; palm branches. What other symbols of Lent can they find in the church? In their own homes? (A crucifix, a Bible; pictures of Jesus' Passion, etc.)

 Faith Journey Activity

Give the children the items you brought and ask them to use them as illustrations of today's lesson. Let them use their imaginations. Hang the posters under the heading, *Lent Begins*.

• Lesson Two • Saying "Yes" to Jesus

"From the time of the apostles, becoming a Christian has been accomplished by a journey and initiation in several stages. This journey can be covered rapidly or slowly, but certain essential elements will always have to be present: proclamation of the Word, acceptance of the Gospel entailing conversion, profession of faith, Baptism itself, the outpouring of the Holy Spirit, and admission to Eucharistic communion" (*Catechism of the Catholic Church*, #1229).

Leader Meditation
A reading from Matthew 4:18-22.

 Preparation

You will need a piece of paper in the shape of a circle, mounted on a piece of cardboard. It should be the size of a button, approximately 2" in diameter. Also, you will need drawing utensils for each child, safety pins, tacky glue, and any pictures you might find useful in illustrating the children's way to follow Jesus.

 Scripture Sharing

Read Matthew 14:22-33, "Jesus Walks on the Water." Discuss how hard it must have been for Peter to step out into the deep water to follow Jesus. Jesus says "Come" to each of us. Discuss times when it is not easy to say "yes" to Jesus' invitation.

 Discussion

• Read or let the children read aloud, *Jesus is Calling*. Discuss the reasons the men in the stories said "no" to Jesus. Is there anything that stands in the way of *their* "yes" at this time? What can be done to help?

• Read *Twelve Who Walked With Jesus* as a group. Choose two to read the Andrew and Peter part, two to read for James and John, two for Philip and Thomas, etc. Read the last two verses together.

• Reread the story of Jesus' call to his apostles one stanza at a time. Discuss: How would it feel to be Peter and Andrew? James and John? Do you think it was hard to leave their families and their business to follow Jesus? Could you have done it?

• The children are preparing to say "yes" to Jesus. Are they ready? What does Jesus expect from them? Discuss ways to live as Christian children.

• Ask: How will other people know that you are following Jesus? Will you change enough for others to see?

 Faith Journey Activity

Have the children illustrate their own way to follow Jesus on the buttons. They can draw themselves in prayer, serving others, going to Church, etc. Offer suggestions, but let them choose their own route. Attach the safety pins to the back of the button with tacky glue. After they have dried, pin their buttons under the heading *Choosing Jesus*.

• Lesson Three •
Looking at Myself

The Scrutinies

"The education of the conscience is a lifelong task. From the earliest years, it awakens the child to the knowledge and practice of the interior law recognized by conscience. Prudent education teaches virtue; it prevents or cures fear, selfishness and pride, resentment arising from guilt, and feelings of complacency, born of human weakness and faults. The education of the conscience guarantees freedom and engenders peace of heart" (*Catechism of the Catholic Church,* #1784; see also #1786–1794).

Leader Meditation
A reading from Matthew 21:28-32.

 Preparation

Believing in Jesus is all about love. We follow Jesus with our hearts. For your activity today, you will make heart puzzles. Cut out four cardboard hearts. Make it so that each piece is part of a larger heart. Write "Love Mends All Hearts" on each heart. Take large-sized bandages and write the word "love" on them. When the pieces are complete, tape the bandages across the heart.

 **Scripture Sharing**

Read the "Parable of the Two Sons," Matthew 21:28-31. Discuss the difference between *saying* you will do something and *actually* doing it. We are called to follow Jesus with our whole selves, not just with our voices.

 Discussion

• Read the section on good guilt and bad guilt. Give the children time to think about and list times they have felt guilty. Discuss individual answers with the class only if the child feels comfortable with this. Also, make sure that *you* participate in this activity.

• Discuss the three things that may make you feel guilty. Take them one at a time, and encourage the children to add their personal comments and experiences.

• Have the children take turns reading the stories under the heading *What is Sin?* Ask them, "Have you ever done anything accidently that made you feel guilty?" "Have you ever made a mistake that made you feel guilty?"

• Read the stories under *How You Can Love God and Others.* Discuss ways they personally love God and others — at home, in the classroom, on the playground, in their prayers. What is the secret of not sinning? (Love God and love one another.)

 Faith Journey Activity

Group the children in threes. Give them their heart puzzles to put together. Discuss a time they healed a broken heart with love. Ask them to draw/illustrate this time. Then glue each heart to a sheet of red construction paper and tape them under the heading, *Love Cannot Sin.*

· Lesson Four ·
The Nicene Creed

"Whoever says 'I believe' says 'I pledge myself to what *we* believe.' Communion in faith needs a common language of faith, normative for all and uniting all in the same confession of faith."…"*The Niceno-Constantinopolitan* or *Nicene Creed* draws its great authority from the fact that it stems from the first two ecumenical Councils (in 325 and 381). It remains common to all the great Churches of both East and West to this day" (*Catechism of the Catholic Church,* #185, #195; see #186–197).

Leader Meditation

A reading from Matthew 21:28-32.

In preparation for today's lesson, read over the Nicene Creed, thought by thought. Establish, in your heart, your faith in the expressed truth found in each phrase. Take time to *feel* the thoughts. Prepare to share the full glory of the prayer with the children.

● Preparation

Make up "flash cards" with the sections of the Creed, as broken down on page two of the children's leaflets. Number the cards in order, leaving the backs of the cards blank. Collect or create the following images from greeting cards or magazines. Include: Creation; Jesus and Mary; the crucifixion; a Holy Spirit symbol; and a church.

● Scripture Sharing

Read to the children, Romans 10:9-11. Explain that every time we say the Creed at Mass, we are confessing our faith in Jesus. Even though we know in our hearts that Jesus is our Lord, God wants us to "confess with our lips" all those things Jesus taught us, all that we truly believe with faith. Follow this reading by reading the Creed together from their leaflets.

Discussion

• Explain to the children that the Creed is our "Profession of Faith." Everything we believe in about God — Father, Son, and Spirit — and about the Church, is affirmed in the Creed. Give examples.

• Pass the Creed cards out to the children. If you have more than five children, choose teams to share cards; less than five, allow some children to read more than one card. As you call out the numbers, have the children read their section of the Creed.

• As each child reads his or her section, stop and discuss what that section means. Let the child who reads the card open and lead the discussion.

• As a class, compose a thank you prayer, for our faith and for God's love, using all the truths found in the Creed.

Faith Journey Activity

Show the children the pictures you brought. Ask them to turn in their Creed cards. Shuffle and return them. Now ask the children to choose the picture that is mentioned in their section of the Creed. Punch a hole into the top of the card and tie a piece of yarn to it. Then have them turn their cards over and paste their chosen picture on the back of the card. Hang these under the heading, *The Creed.* Or take a hanger and attach a sign which reads "the Creed." Punch holes on the bottom of the sign large enough to hang the Creed cards from it. The end result is a Creed Mobile.

• Lesson Five •
The Way
of the Cross

"The prayer of the Church venerates and honors the *Heart of Jesus* just as it invokes his most holy name. It adores the incarnate Word and his Heart which, out of love for [us], he allowed to be pierced by our sins. Christian prayer loves to follow *the way of the cross* in the Savior's steps. The stations from the Praetorium to Golgotha and the tomb trace the way of Jesus, who by his holy Cross has redeemed the world" (*Catechism of the Catholic Church,* #2669; see also #1674).

Leader Meditation

Slowly and deliberately read any one of the passages describing Jesus' passion and death, Matthew 26; Mark 15; Luke 22; or John 18:12—19:24. Allow yourself to become a part of the crowd, witness to all that is happening. Let your heart pray in thanksgiving to God for giving us a love so great and complete.

 ## Preparation

You will need a cardboard or wooden cross, approximately two feet high. Cut out smaller crosses, several for each child. You will also need crayons or markers and tape for the smaller crosses.

Scripture Sharing

Read one or all the passion and death passages you chose for your meditation. If your children are very young, paraphrase the passage or use a children's Bible. Keep an eye on their reactions. If they feel moved, encourage them to share their feelings about the reading and about Jesus.

 ## Discussion

• If possible, take the children into the Church to do the Stations of the Cross together. Have them bring their leaflets so they can say the prayer with each Station after you read the opening explanation. If the Church is not available to you, do the prayers without Stations, using the leaflets or any children's Stations of the Cross.

• Discuss the small prayers they read with the Stations. These prayers are meant to help the child relate some of their own problems with Jesus' sufferings. Do these prayers help him or her identify with Jesus? Do they help him or her believe that Jesus cares about their worries and sufferings?

• Discuss some of the suffering people in the world: the hungry in the Third World, those in countries where war is a constant threat, people who are discriminated against because of color, religion, or gender. What do these things have to do with Jesus? Jesus cares about everyone. Remember his words: "Whatever you do to the least of my people, you do to me." When we hurt, he hurts.

• Ask why Jesus chose to die. Help them to understand that this was Jesus' way to show love for all of us. By dying on the cross, he took on our crosses too. Because Jesus died willingly for us, we are now officially adopted as children of God.

• Discuss the question, "How much would you be willing to suffer for a friend or a loved one?"

Faith Journey Activity

Hang the larger cross you brought in under the heading *The Way of the Cross*. Pass out the small crosses, as many as the children want. Ask them to write their names on the front of the paper crosses. On the back, they should list sufferings in the world or in their lives. By hanging their suffering on the cross with Jesus, they are asking Jesus to share their pain.

• Lesson Six •
The Lord's Prayer

"When Jesus prays he is already teaching us how to pray. His prayer to his Father is the theological path (the path of faith, hope, and charity) of our prayer to God. But the Gospel also gives us Jesus' explicit teaching on prayer. Like a wise teacher he takes hold of us where we are and leads us progressively toward the Father. Addressing the crowds following him, Jesus builds on what they already know of prayer from the Old Covenant and opens to them the newness of the coming Kingdom. Then he reveals this newness to them in parables. Finally, he will speak openly of the Father and the Holy Spirit to his disciples who will be the teachers of prayer in his Church" (*Catechism of the Catholic Church*, #2607).

Leader Meditation
A reading from Matthew 6:7-13.

Preparation

You will need an 8 ¹/₂" x 11" sheet of white construction paper for each child. You will also need scissors, pencils, markers, and tape.

Scripture Sharing

Read or tell in your own words Jesus' promise to those who pray, Matthew 6:8. Encourage discussion about prayer and God's answer. Do they believe that God always answers prayers? How are they answered? What if God says "no"? How do they feel about "unanswered" prayers? Let them know that sometimes prayers that we think are unanswered *are* answered.

Discussion

• Go over the Lord's Prayer once with the children. Take some time to do the suggested prayer ideas from the leaflet.

• Have the children close their eyes while you repeat the prayer again. If they already know the prayer, invite them to pray with you.

• While their eyes are still closed, read the section *After You Have Prayed*. Give them time to think about the prayer and be with Jesus.

• Ask the questions listed on page two of the leaflet. Allow the discussion to flow freely until you are certain each child is satisfied with the answers, then go on to the next question.

• Discuss temptations the children have faced or might face one day. Ask how they handle temptation. Refer to the story of Jesus in the desert, Matthew 4:1-11 or Luke 4:1-13.

Faith Journey Activity

Fold the construction paper in half lengthwise. Have each child trace his or her partner's hand on the folded paper. The straight part of the hand near the small finger should be held flush against the fold of the paper. On the inside of the folded hands, ask the children to write a short prayer, or rewrite the Lord's Prayer in contemporary language. Then they can decorate them any way they'd like. Tape the finished praying hands under the heading *The Lord's Prayer*. These can be attached to their classroom maps.

• Lesson Seven •
Holy Week

"Therefore *Easter* is not simply one feast among others, but the 'Feast of feasts,' the 'Solemnity of solemnities,' just as the Eucharist is the 'Sacrament of sacraments' (the Great Sacrament). St. Athanasius calls Easter 'the Great Sunday' and the Eastern Churches call Holy Week 'the Great Week.' The mystery of the Resurrection, in which Christ crushed death, permeates with its powerful energy our old time, until all is subjected to him" (*Catechism of the Catholic Church*, #1169).

Leader Meditation

A Sponsor's Personal Prayer

Me! A spiritual companion for fledgling faith! Loving Spirit of God, I tremble inside. I hold fast to you, great Giver of Life, offering my prayer of thanksgiving for this very special gift, and my prayer of supplication for the graces needed to be worthy of it. Can anything be more important than being a good sponsor for one who is about to enter your Church? Overwhelmed by the honor of it, and frightened by the responsibility of it, I say, "Yes," my Lord. It is not clear why you have chosen me, but you clearly have. So I will travel this journey of faith with the one who called my name. As we move along your Way, we sense that the path leads to everywhere, and to nowhere. We two will share our stories, and will learn more of you as we learn more of ourselves, through the eyes of always-newly-becoming Christian witness. Grant to both of us — and to all of us — the grace to touch each other's hearts with your tender mercy and your steadfast love. Amen

Preparation

This is an important time for the children, one they will want to share with family and friends. For your activity, have several 8 ¹/₂" x 11" sheets of white paper, folded in half — for each child. These will be used to make invitations to the Easter celebration. Have items on hand to decorate their invitations: stickers, pictures depicting Easter, glitter glue, markers, etc. Take down their *Faith Journey Map* papers and staple them into booklets as before.

Scripture Sharing

Rather than choosing a Scripture this week, read *The Giving Tree* by Shel Silverstein. The tree is like Jesus — he gave all that he had in his life and then continued to give when his life was over. Encourage a discussion.

Discussion

• Read *Hail to the King* from the children's leaflet. Discuss your parish's celebration of Palm Sunday. Allow time to answer and discuss the questions following the short passage.

• Read *The Passion Story* from the children's leaflet. Ask what this story reminds them of (the Stations of the Cross). Allow time for them to answer and discuss the questions following the passage.

• Read the complete explanations of the Easter Triduum. Explain how these days will be celebrated in your parish.

• Use the rest of your time to review and prepare the children for the sacraments they will be receiving at the Easter Vigil.

Faith Journey Activity

Set out the items for the children to make their invitations. Explain that they will be giving these invitations to friends and relatives. Go over wording ideas in advance for the invitation. Take pictures of the kids creating their invitations. Attach them under the heading *Holy Week*.

· Lesson Eight · Catechumenate Retreat Day

"From the time of the apostles, becoming a Christian has been accomplished by a journey and initiation in several stages. This journey can be covered rapidly or slowly, but certain essential elements will always have to be present: the proclamation of the Word, acceptance of the Gospel entailing conversion, profession of faith, Baptism itself, the outpouring of the Holy Spirit, and admission to Eucharistic communion" (*Catechism of the Catholic Church,* #1229; see also #1230).

Leader Meditation
A reading from Psalm 92:1-4.

Preparation

The retreat journey is based on the Easter Vigil Liturgy of the Word in order to help the candidates and catechumens participate more deeply in the Mass and sacraments of initiation. Involve the children as much as possible. Select songs the children enjoy. Since you will plan this day with the RCIA leaders, allow time for the children to work on their projects.

For your final activity after the retreat, you will need plastic foam wreath forms, Easter grass, and small items to glue onto their Easter wreaths: small gold crosses, Easter eggs, bunnies, chicks, or any other signs of new life (you can find most of these in the craft section of any department store). Write the words "He Is Risen" and glue onto cardboard just large enough to fit behind the wreaths so the words show through the center.

Scripture Sharing

Gather with the adults for the Scripture readings. After the readings, take the children to a separate room or space to review the readings. Take time to discuss the readings if there are any questions. Follow this by answering the questions from the leaflet.

Discussion

• Read the quote from the first reading found on page one of the leaflet. Have the children answer the questions found after the section "Are you ready?" Discuss their answers, especially any doubts that may surface at this time.

• Follow the same procedure with each of the readings, reading the quote, discussing the reading and allowing them time to answer the questions in the leaflet.

Faith Journey Activity

After the retreat, allow time for the children to make their Easter wreaths. Cover the wreaths with glue and attach Easter grass. Glue on the symbols. Then glue the whole thing to the *He Is Risen* cardboard and trim the cardboard to fit the wreath.

Make sure you create a sample wreath. Place that under the heading *A New Journey*.

• Lesson One •
Conversion: A
Lifelong Process

"'A *parish* is a definite community of the Christian faithful established on a stable basis within a particular church; the pastoral care of the parish is entrusted to a pastor as its own shepherd under the authority of the diocesan bishop.' It is the place where all the faithful can be gathered together for the Sunday celebration of the Eucharist. The parish initiates the Christian people into the ordinary expression of the liturgical life: it gathers them together in this celebration; it teaches Christ's saving doctrine; it practices the charity of the Lord in good works and...love" (*Catechism of the Catholic Church*, #2179).

Leader Meditation
A reading from Hebrews 2:1-4.

 Preparation

For this section, you will need maps with the following titles: Conversion, The Laity; Special Gifts; Family Life; Discernment. This week's suggested activity is a mobile displaying times when Jesus joins us on our journey. Cut out simple forms for a dove, Bible, Church, the bread & wine, and folded hands. Punch a small hole in the top of each form. Print the words "Spirit," "Word of God," "Our Parish Family," "the Eucharist," and "Prayer" on the board. Prepare a 10" strip of heavy cardboard with the words "Growing Together"and punch five holes at two-inch intervals. You will need different lengths of yarn to hang your figures.

 Scripture Sharing

Read or tell in your own words one of the passages telling of the call of the apostles, Matthew 4:18-22, Mark 1:16-20, Luke 5:1-11. Explain that

Jesus is saying the same thing to them: "Come, Follow Me." They are setting out to follow Jesus with their parish family.

 Discussion

• Using the section *A Time to Remember,* review what has been learned about Jesus. Give them time to answer the questions on the leaflet, then discuss their answers.

• Move on to the section *Keep on Growing.* Ask what they remember about the stories mentioned in this section.

• Review the story of the coming of the Holy Spirit with the children, then give them time to answer the questions in the leaflet.

• As members of God's family, the children will be guided by the Holy Spirit to become active Christians. What can they do for others to show their love for God?

 Faith Journey Activity

Place the items you cut out on the work table. Ask each child to choose one item and label it according to one of the words on the board. Using the lengths of yarn and your "Growing Together" banner, create a mobile of ways Jesus will lead them and help them to grow in the faith. Display a sample mobile under the heading *Conversion.*

• Lesson Two • The Laity: Called to Build God's Kingdom

"The very differences which the Lord has willed to put between the members of his body serve its unity and mission. For 'in the Church there is diversity of ministry but unity of mission. To the apostles and their successors Christ has entrusted the office of teaching, sanctifying, and governing in his name and by his power. But the laity are made to share in the priestly, prophetical, and kingly office of Christ; they have therefore, in the Church and in the world, their own assignment in the mission of the whole People of God.' Finally, 'from both groups [hierarchy and laity] there exist Christian faithful who are consecrated to God in their own special manner and serve the salvific mission of the Church through the profession of the evangelical counsels'" (*Catechism of the Catholic Church,* #873; see also #814–1937).

Leader Meditation
A reading from 1 Corinthians 12:14-18, 26.

 ## Preparation

Your suggested activity this week is a poster illustrating ways the children will choose to serve the Body of Christ. Across the top of the poster, write the words, "We are all one Body." Using a ruler and a bright-colored marker, divide the poster into as many sections as you have children. Write one child's name in each section. If you have only one or two children, divide the poster into four sections labeled: *At Home, At School, At Church, In My Neighborhood.*

Or, draw an outline of a body. Assign sections to the children.

 ## Scripture Sharing

Read or tell in your own words the passage outlining the Body of Christ — One Body with Many Members, 1 Corinthians 12:12-31. We are all members of Christ's Body, and we all have different (and very special) ways to serve that Body.

 ## Discussion

• Draw a simple body figure on the board, leaving off details such as eyes, ears, etc. Add the details one at a time. Each time, ask the children, for example, "What purpose do our eyes (ears, hands, feet, etc.) serve?"

• What would happen to us if our ears didn't hear, our eyes didn't see, our feet couldn't walk?

• We are all members of Christ's Body, the Church. Each of us should help the Body be whole. How can we, as members of Christ's body, help those who have a physical disability or are hearing or visually impaired?

• Go through the leaflet with the children, helping them to discern special ways they can serve the Spiritual Body of Christ at home, church, school, in their neighborhoods.

• Explain to them that as they are physically building this activity, it's the same way we build God's kingdom, piece by piece, person by person.

Faith Journey Activity

Place the poster board on the work table. Give each child a section on which to illustrate one way he or she will serve the Body of Christ. If you have only one or two children, work together to discern and illustrate ways to serve the Body of Christ at home, church, school, and in the neighborhood.

Or, using the body outline, make sure there are enough parts for your group. Let the children either draw or collect images that depict serving the body of Christ. These should be placed in their designated sections. When complete, the body should look like a collage. Attach this under the heading *The Laity.*

• Lesson Three •
Your Special Gifts

"The Holy Spirit is 'the principle of every vital and truly saving action in each part of the Body.' He works in many ways to build up the whole Body in charity: by God's Word 'which is able to build you up'; by Baptism, through which he forms Christ's Body; by the sacraments, which give growth and healing to Christ's members; by 'the grace of the apostles, which holds first place among his gifts'; by the virtues, which make us act according to what is good; finally, by the many special graces (called 'charisms'), by which he makes the faithful 'fit and ready to undertake various tasks and offices for the renewal and building up of the Church'" (*Catechism of the Catholic Church*, #798; see also #799–800, #2003).

Leader Meditation
A reading from 1 Corinthians 12:4-11.

 ## Preparation

This week the children will make "Spiritual gift" cards, illustrating gifts they have and ways they will use them for the Church. You will need one 8 1/2" x 11" sheet of drawing paper folded in half for each child. You will also need markers and different colored yarn.

 ## Scripture Sharing

Read the passage from the *Leader Meditation* to the children. Encourage a discussion to ascertain that the children understand that they, along with all other members of Christ's body, were given special gifts to use in God's service.

 ## Discussion

• Using the explanations offered in the children's leaflet, go over each gift one at a time. Allow the children time to answer the questions either in writing or as a part of your discussion.

• If anyone hasn't been able to identify a personal gift, ask the group to think about that person and name one gift they believe he or she possesses. Share with the group those special gifts you have noticed in each of them.

• Once the children's gifts are recognized, discuss ways these gifts can be used to help and serve others for God. (A child with a happy spirit can cheer up those who are sad; a child with the gift of wisdom can help other children in the group; a child with the gift of healing can visit the sick; etc.)

 ## Faith Journey Activity

Give one blank card to each child. Instruct the child to write "God's Gift to Me" on the front of the card. They can write the name of their gift or illustrate it in some way. Inside, instruct them to write, "My Gift to God." Here, they are to illustrate some way(s) they can use their gifts to serve God. Create sample cards in different shapes, sizes, etc. Display those on your map under the heading *Special Gifts*.

• Lesson Four • Family Life

"'The Christian family constitutes a specific revelation and realization of ecclesial communion, and for this reason it can and should be called a *domestic church*' It is a community of faith, hope, and charity; it assumes singular importance in the Church, as is evident in the New Testament" (*Catechism of the Catholic Church,* #2204; see also #2205).

Leader Meditation
A reading from Colossians 3:12-17.

 ## Preparation

This week's activity is a personal "family tree" for each child to bring home and finish. Copy the tree pattern onto an 8 ¹/₂" x 11" sheet of heavy paper. Make one for each child in your group. You will need some bark or burlap, as well as markers or crayons to decorate the tree. Also, cut out circles from construction paper to glue onto the branches. If the children have some old family pictures, they can be used too.

 ## Scripture Sharing

Read Colossians 3:18-21. Encourage a discussion about ways that each family member can follow these directives in the name of love.

 ## Discussion

• Read *Sharing Jesus Stories* together. Ask them to select a favorite Jesus story and act it out. Make sure everyone has a turn.
• Using the leaflet ideas, discuss ways families can make going to Church a fun time. Ask about special things their families do on Sundays.
• Read *Pray Together at Home.* Ask the children to share a time when their families pray together. They can bring their leaflets home to share other prayer times with their families.
• Discuss name saints. What do they know about their name saint? Discuss the patron saint of your parish and why that saint is a good choice for a parish family.

 ## Faith Journey Activity

Give each child a family tree picture. Let them decorate the trees, using the bark and/or burlap, or simply coloring them. Leave enough room on the bottom for their names. Set a stack of circles on each table and show the children what to do. Then ask them to fill in those people whose names they know and to bring their family trees home so their parents can help them finish them. It may be easier for them if you do a sample tree and place it under the heading *Family Life.*

• Lesson Five •
Your Prayer Life

"Prayer and *Christian life* are *inseparable,* for they concern the same love and the same renunciation, proceeding from love; the same filial and loving conformity with the Father's plan of love; the same transforming union in the Holy Spirit who conforms us more and more to Christ Jesus; the same love for all [people], the love with which Jesus has loved us. 'Whatever you ask the Father in my name, he [will] give it to you. This I command you, to love one another'" (*Catechism of the Catholic Church,* #2745, see also #2688).

Leader Meditation
A reading from John 16:23-27.

 ## Preparation

For this week's activity, purchase or create a small spiral notebook for each child. These will become their "prayer books." Cut out pieces of white cardboard to fit over the fronts of the books. You will need glue sticks, markers or crayons, and other decorative objects for the children to illustrate the covers.

 ## Scripture Sharing

Read Matthew 6:1-9. After reading verse 9, "Pray then in this way:," say the Lord's Prayer together.

 ## Discussion

• Ask the children why they think Jesus asked the people to pray to God in secret. Does this mean we should not pray together? Read and discuss Matthew 18:20: "For where two or three are gathered in my name, I am there among them."

• Read *A Love Connection to God* together. Encourage a discussion about times when the children like to pray and times when they find prayer difficult.

• Read the short passages mentioned in *Getting to Know God Through Scripture.* Have the children answer the questions in that section and discuss their answers.

• Encourage the children to share their feelings about prayers that were not answered. This can be a tough discussion. Be aware of ways God answers our prayers without us knowing it. Remind them that sometimes parents have to say "no" to their children. Why? They, like God, know that not everything we ask for is good for us.

• Read or have the children read the story, *Jimmy's Surprise.* Was Jimmy's prayer answered? How?

 ## Faith Journey Activity

Give the children their notebooks. Let them decorate the cardboard covers and glue them over the front page. Discuss the many types of prayers. Give them time to write a prayer in one of the discussed formats. Assure them that anything they write will be private. Encourage them to take the books home and add any prayers they want to record.

• Lesson Six •
Discernment

"Faced with a moral choice, conscience can make either a right judgment in accordance with reason and the divine law or, on the contrary, an erroneous judgment that departs from them. To this purpose, [we] strive to interpret the data of experience and the signs of the times assisted by the virtue of prudence, by the advice of competent people, and by the help of the Holy Spirit and his gifts" (*Catechism of the Catholic Church*, #1786, #1788; see also #1787–1802).

Leader Meditation
A reading from Hebrews 13:7-9.

 Preparation

Cut out a set of stairs, one for each step found in the leaflet, leaving room for an example. You will need seven 3" x 5" file cards for each child. Punch two holes in the top of each card. The children will need two pieces of yarn to tie their cards together and pencils, pens, or markers to write on the steps.

 Scripture Sharing

Rather than a Scripture this week, read *When You Don't Know What to Do* from the first page of the leaflet. Encourage a discussion about Joey's decision.

 Discussion

• Ask the children to put themselves in Joey's place. What would they decide?

• Discuss times when the children had a difficult time making a decision. What did they do? Who, if anyone, helped them make their decision?

• Print out the seven steps to decision-making on the board.

• Go over each step with the children, one at a time. Allow time for them to do the exercises on their leaflets. Encourage discussion.

• At the fourth and fifth steps, ask the children what they decided and how they feel about their decision.

• At steps six and seven, discuss how they will act on their decision. Allow time for a silent prayer of thanks for God's help in their decision-making.

 Faith Journey Activity

Give each child seven cards and two pieces of yarn. Let them string the yarn through their cards and tie them. Ask them to copy the steps from the board onto the file cards and number them, and to list an example under each step.

Encourage the children to keep their cards in a safe place and use them whenever they have a difficult decision to make. Under the heading *Discernment,* create a set of stairs using the steps. This is something for the children to use as reference.

• Lesson Seven •
Holiness

"'All Christians in any state or walk of life are called to the fullness of Christian life and to the perfection of charity.' All are called to holiness: 'Be perfect, as your heavenly Father is perfect.' In order to reach this perfection the faithful should use the strength dealt out to them by Christ's gift, so that...doing the will of the Father in everything, they may wholeheartedly devote themselves to the glory of God and to the service of their neighbor. Thus the holiness of the People of God will grow in fruitful abundance, as is clearly shown in the history of the Church through the lives of so many saints" (*Catechism of the Catholic Church*, #2013).

Leader Meditation
A reading from Romans 8:28-30.

Preparation

Using a large-sized sheet of white paper, prepare a simple map with five stops (you can mark the stops with Xs). A dotted line should circle around the stops, touching each one, and finish where it began. The children will need crayons or markers to draw in their stopping places.

Scripture Sharing

Read John 15:12-17 to the children. Discuss what it means to be a "friend" to Jesus. Being a friend to Jesus is the best way to be holy.

Discussion

• After the children have written the names of three holy people they know, encourage a discussion about what makes a person holy. Why did they choose the particular people they chose? Do they consider themselves to be holy?

• Holiness means to follow Jesus in everything we say and do. Discuss things Jesus did that they can imitate: Jesus helped the sick, told stories about God, cared about people, prayed often, taught others to pray, told us to love one another, loved the poor, suffered for God, etc.

• Have each child write down one thing he or she will do this week to be more like Jesus: help at home, visit someone who's sick, collect food for the poor, etc. If possible, plan a class holiness project along those same lines.

• Read the *Create Your Own Holiness Treasure Map* section, pointing out all the places where they can discover their holiness. Explain that they will be making treasure maps of their own.

Faith Journey Activity

Pass out the maps you prepared. Go over the holiness stops, one at a time. Give them time to illustrate that stop on their maps (church, home, neighborhood, classroom, playground, and family). Keep the discussion going as they complete their maps.

• Lesson Eight • Evangelization

"'Thus, every person, through these gifts given to [each], is at once the witness and the living instrument of the mission of the Church itself 'according to the measure of Christ's bestowal'" (*Catechism of the Catholic Church*, #913).

Leader Meditation
A reading from Acts 11:19-24.

 Preparation

You will need a piece of white poster board to make your "trail of love" for this lesson. From different colored construction paper, cut out several hearts of different sizes. You will also need tape and markers of contrasting colors for the hearts.

 Scripture Sharing

Read or tell the children in your own words the Scripture passage used as your meditation. Before beginning your reading, explain that this is one story of how the disciples were able to share their faith and help the Church to grow. As the people listened and believed, they joined with other Christians in the Church of Christ.

 Discussion

• Read *Step One — Witness Christ* from the children's leaflets. Discuss ways they can be witnesses to Jesus just by being loving and kind to others — especially at Mass.

• Read *Step Two — Share the Faith*. What stories of Jesus would they like to share with their friends, neighbors, and family members? This is another way they can lead people to Jesus.

• Read *Step Three — Offer the Love of Jesus*. Discuss some ways we can share Jesus' love with others? Who do they know who needs to know that God loves them?

• Read *Step Four — Fight Injustice*. Discuss how would they feel if others were laughing at them or treating them cruelly? Can they name one way to love Jesus by making sure everyone is treated fairly?

• Read *Step Five — Live the Gospel of Jesus*. Discuss the quotations listed one at a time. How can they follow each of these sayings?

 Faith Journey Activity

Give each child several hearts. Using the five steps listed on the leaflet, have them write one way they will share Jesus' love on each heart. Tape the hearts onto the poster. Display the poster where others in the Church can see it.

Or have the children write and illustrate a story about ways they will share Jesus' love. This should be done on heart-shaped paper, no more than two hearts per child. If there are enough children, position the hearts to spell "Jesus" on the poster.